are you crazy?

18 scientific quizzes to test yourself

andrew n. williams

A Perigee Book

THE BERKLEY PUBLISHING GROUP
Published by the Penguin Group
Penguin Group (USA) Inc.
375 Hudson Street, New York, New York 10014, USA
Penguin Group (Canada), 10 Alcorn Avenue, Toronto, Ontario M4V 3B2, Canada
(a division of Pearson Penguin Canada Inc.)
Penguin Books Ltd., 80 Strand, London WC2R 0RL, England
Penguin Group Ireland, 25 St. Stephen's Green, Dublin 2, Ireland (a division of Penguin Books Ltd.)
Penguin Group (Australia), 250 Camberwell Road, Camberwell, Victoria 3124, Australia
(a division of Pearson Australia Group Pty. Ltd.)
Penguin Books India Pvt. Ltd., 11 Community Centre, Panchsheel Park, New Delhi—110 017, India
Penguin Group (NZ), Cnr. Airborne and Rosedale Roads, Albany, Auckland 1310, New Zealand
(a division of Pearson New Zealand Ltd.)
Penguin Books (South Africa) (Pty.) Ltd., 24 Sturdee Avenue, Rosebank, Johannesburg 2196,
South Africa

Penguin Books Ltd., Registered Offices: 80 Strand, London WC2R 0RL, England

PRINTING HISTORY
Perigee trade paperback edition / July 2005

PERIGEE is a registered trademark of Penguin Group (USA) Inc.
The "P" design is a trademark belonging to Penguin Group (USA) Inc.

Library of Congress Cataloging-in-Publication Information

Williams, Andrew N.
   Are you crazy? : 18 scientific quizzes to test yourself / Andrew N. Williams.
      p.   cm.
   Includes index.
   ISBN 0-399-53158-0
   1. Personality tests.   2. Self-evaluation.   I. Title: 18 scientific quizzes to test yourself.
   II. Title: Eighteen scientific quizzes to test yourself.   III. Title.

BF698.5.W545   2005
155.2'83—dc22

                                                                      2004058505

PRINTED IN THE UNITED STATES OF AMERICA

10   9   8   7   6   5   4   3   2

This one is for my brothers: Ian and Norman,
constant reminders of Darwin's theory . . .
—ANW

This one is for my brothers! Robby and Scotty,
who made growing up so much fun!
—BJ

contents

acknowledgments

A book like this is not written by one person. This book is at the point of a vast pyramid of research. I have plowed through hundreds of research articles, written by thousands of professors and professionals, many with a lifetime devoted to specific areas of the mind. Most of their studies involved testing many individuals. Literally tens of thousands of people have taken tests and contributed to our knowledge of psychology. In that sense, this book was very easy to write as I just had to snip off the most interesting bits of mental health research.

Of course sewing together a quilt made of many bits is not easy. It takes organization, planning, forethought—all qualities of my tremendous assistant, Kathie Weber. Thanks Kathie!

Although I love words, I have always worked in the social sciences, and I am more familiar with reading esoteric psychology texts than literature. Cindy Rolfes has been remarkable in assisting me translate technical terms into readable English. Cindy's fresh outlook and easy style has made this book a joy.

The topics are fun, the results are interesting, but wow, those cartoons are brilliant. Buck Jones from Des Moines, Iowa did a fantastic job with his humorous illustrations.

Navigating the world of publishing requires a specialist. Madeleine Morel of 2M Communications is everything an agent should be. Madeleine's knowledge, diligence, and inspiration helped transform an idea into this book. My superlative agent introduced me to a wonderful editor. Thank you to Perigee's Adrienne Schultz for your foresight, enthusiasm, and patience, Adrienne's vision of this work helped shape it into the book in your hands. And thanks to Kathryn McHugh for getting this project started. You have to love an editor who gets all excited over a word like "triskaidekaphobia" (you'll find it in the Fear chapter.)

I've tried to keep the statistics hidden, but there is a great deal of number crunching behind choosing good tests. Thank you, Professor Jean Opsomer, for the statistical advice. And finally, thanks to the people who supported this colossal effort by sharing their tales of weirdness, comments, kisses, and cheese sandwiches: Christine, Jack, David, Pete, James, Kathleen, Sharon, Russ, Martha, Palvi, Pavan, Allie, Deb, Forrest, Emily, and Grace.

preface

What a crazy world we live in. You can't listen to the news or read a paper without realizing there is an abundance of oddballs in the world. A couple of years ago, I read that police in Japan arrested a man for stealing shoes. Women's shoes. 444 shoes. All for the left foot. My dental hygienist breaks out in a cold sweat if the peas roll into her mashed potatoes on her dinner plate. (Don't even ask about gravy!) And we've all heard stories about some "mother of the year" who is slowly, secretly killing her daughter, just to get the attention. Where do all these peculiar people come from?

I am an experimental psychologist. Over the past twenty years, I learned that there is a secret behind every front door in America. Hidden behind the smiles of normalcy and obscured by a façade of etiquette, lay quirks, secrets, and peculiarities. Each of us has our idiosyncrasies: those small curious behaviors that add personality and character to daily life. Every household has its own taboos and special requirements for family members that are impossible to discern from the exterior. But, once you get to know someone, really get intimate with them, and peel back those layers of decorum, you learn about their mind-jarring oddities. And there comes a point in every relationship where you shake your head in disbelief, and ask, *Are You Crazy?*

There is a massive range for "normal" behavior. Some people fall smack-dab in the middle of the normal range, others skirt the outer edge of average, and then many of us dot the abnormal area—at least for one or two small deeds. Perhaps you enjoy it when your partner gives you a little spank on the tush. Does that make you a masochist? How many wallops does it take before you are one? When does a habit become a quirk? When does a hobby become an obsession? What separates being particular from being peculiar? Where is the line between individualism and downright odd? Everyone has some weird uncle or a curious aunt. Will you become one of these? *Are You Crazy?* answers these questions.

I am going to take you on a tour of the hidden, dark recesses of the mind. We are going to visit many places. We are going to see, firsthand, what makes odd people tick. We are going to peek in bedroom windows, open the fridge, and listen at doors. Not only will we learn about others, we will learn about you. There are some great tests in *Are You Crazy?* Not only are they fun, amusing, insightful, and revealing, they are scientific, university-developed quizzes designed to unlock the secrets of your personality.

The chapters in this book are laid out like two strangers meeting. The visitors get to know each other in Chapter One, then they discuss their relationship needs. In Chapter Three, they decide to go out for dinner and a drink, the relationship blossoms so they have lots of gratuitous sex, they fall in love, and discuss their fears and foibles. By the end of the book, they have grown to depend on each other and live happily ever after in their own quirky world.

I have found where all these crazy people come from; every home in the country. Take my hand now, we will visit them and learn, *Are You Crazy?*

—ANW

JULY 2005

1.

getting to know you, getting to know all about you: discovering yourself

Everyone is crazy except you and me, and I'm not always sure about you. —MY TINY IRISH GRANDMOTHER

Before we get to know you, let me say a bit about this book. It is your personal escort to quirks, oddities, and bizarre behavior. It will be your tour guide as we take a stroll around the peculiar corners of the mind. In each chapter, we will make a few stops to complete some fun, easy-to-take questionnaires. These are not magazine quizzes, but actual scientific personality scales developed by top psychologists and psychiatrists. Your thoughtful answers to these questions will enable me to point out the color and sophistication of your personality.

Learning about yourself and about your friends and family is only half of the book; the real value comes from amusing and insightful anecdotes of the eccentricities of others. I'm going to share anecdotes about the secret lives of people. My goal is to give you the chance to take a few steps in the shoes of others.

Perhaps you just can't understand why a little girl would want to pull out all her hair or you are repulsed at the idea of bestiality. These reactions are quite normal. However, the fascination, the draw, of peeking into the minds of others is intoxicating. As you will see, the world would be a very dull place if we did not have a little crazy in all of us. We are not here to poke fun at the mentally ill, but to take a relaxed, open look at fascinating behavior. So, get ready as we embark on a tour of your personality, the bizarre lives of others, and, if we are lucky, we will even catch a glimpse into the weird rules of our society.

Before we get underway, I want to emphasize one final point. This book has been written to entertain and educate. The tests presented are to help you learn about yourself, others, and ideally, to better understand the quirks of people you know—they are not diagnostic tools for those seeking clinical help. If you believe you have an emotional, psychological, or psychiatric problem, please see a competent professional.

Okay, that is who I am and why I'm here, let's get to know you . . .

Narcissism

Messages about loving yourself, being confident, and comfortable in your skin bombard us. We are constantly given mantras like "everyone is special" and "you have to love yourself first." From an early age, classroom teachers use positive reinforcement to bolster the self-image of every student. The importance of having a healthy ego is undeniable, but are we raising our children to think they are so wonderful that they require excessive attention, affirmation, admiration, and adulation? Can we all be that great? Do we get so wrapped up in ourselves that we ignore others? Are we developing into a nation of narcissists?

ARE YOU A NARCISSIST?

We are taught that self-confidence, pride, and assertiveness are admirable traits. So how do you know when you've crossed the line? Psychological experts believe you have Narcissistic Personality Disorder if you answer yes to at least five of the following questions:

Do you exaggerate your accomplishments and talents and feel that everything you do is important?   YES   NO

Do you only associate with other distinguished people and institutions?   YES   NO

Do you frequently fantasize about having power, prestige, brilliance, beauty, or the "perfect" romance?   YES   NO

Do you require excessive and ongoing admiration from others?   YES   NO

Do you feel you deserve special treatment and feel others should comply with your expectations?   YES   NO

Do you exploit others if it will benefit you?   YES   NO

Are you apathetic about the feelings or concerns of others?   YES   NO

Are you envious of other people's accomplishments and material belongings?   YES   NO

Do others describe you as condescending and arrogant?   YES   NO

Narcissists love themselves to the exclusion of others. Narcissistic Personality Disorder gets its name from the ancient Greek story of Narcissus, the handsome young man who caught his reflection in a pond and was so smitten with his own image, he continued to stare until he withered away and died.

Do You Know a Narcissist?

While only about 1 percent of the population is diagnosed with Narcissistic Personality Disorder, millions of Americans operate under the influence of narcissism. Take Paul for example. When Paul interviewed for the midlevel management sales job at A2Z Corporation, he seemed like the perfect candidate. Gregarious, outspoken, confident, and assertive during the interview, this former marine was a shoe-in for the job. Paul's evident charm, enthusiasm for the position, and his head full of ideas seemed like a guaranteed recipe for corporate success. In no time, A2Z Corporation offered Paul the job, and he accepted. He quickly became quite a stud around the office. But, as the weeks passed, Paul became impatient and resentful when management failed to implement all of his suggestions. His employees complained that he overworked them, ignored their ideas, and was condescending and critical of the smallest mistakes. When midlevel managers in other departments received promotions, Paul become envious and bitter, openly criticizing the company's decisions and leadership for not promoting him. A2Z's final decision regarding Paul was to return him to the ranks of the unemployed.

For many demanding and high-profile occupations, some narcissistic traits are helpful, perhaps even crucial, to success. Successful business leaders, politicians, and professional athletes all exhibit some narcissistic qualities. With this personality trait, a little goes a long way. So how can you tell whether you have what it takes to be a captain of industry or if you're destined to be a Captain Bligh of the boardroom? Well, sharpen your pencils, sit down, and take the Narcissist Test to discover if you're likely to forget the old sports adage, there's no "I" in team. (But you can spell "me"!)

Instructions

While you may not have the disorder, we all have some narcissist qualities. Here is a fun chance to examine yourself. This short quiz will give you insights about why you do the things you do. It consists of ten statements and asks how characteristic each one is of your behavior. Just circle the number which best represents your opinion. There are no right or wrong answers. It takes about five minutes to complete. Do not rush. Carefully think about each question, and be honest.

HOW NARCISSISTIC ARE YOU?

Circle the number that corresponds to your feelings or behavior:

	Very Uncharacteristic	Uncharacteristic	Neutral	Characteristic	Very Characteristic
1. I can become absorbed in thinking about my personal affairs, my health, my cares, or my relations to others.	1	2	3	4	5
2. My feelings are easily hurt by ridicule or the slighting remarks of others.	1	2	3	4	5
3. When I enter a room, I often become self-conscious and feel that the eyes of others are upon me.	1	2	3	4	5
4. I dislike sharing the credit of an achievement with others.	1	2	3	4	5
5. I feel I have enough on my hands without worrying about other people's troubles.	1	2	3	4	5
6. I feel I am temperamentally different from most people.	1	2	3	4	5
7. I often interpret the remarks of others in a personal way.	1	2	3	4	5
8. I easily become wrapped up in my own interest and forget the existence of others.	1	2	3	4	5
9. I dislike being with a group unless I know that I am appreciated by at least one of those present.	1	2	3	4	5

10. I am secretly "put out" or annoyed when other people come to me with their troubles, asking me for my time and sympathy.

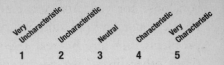

Very Uncharacteristic	Uncharacteristic	Neutral	Characteristic	Very Characteristic
1	2	3	4	5

- -

Hendin, H.M., and Cheek, J.M. (1997). Assessing Hypersensitive Narcissism: A Re-examination of Murray's Narcissism Scale. Journal of Research in Personality, 31, 588-599. Used with permission.

Scoring Your Test

To find your score, simply add the ten numbers you circled and write your score on the line below.

Your Score _____

UNDERSTANDING YOUR SCORE

Your Score	Level of Narcissism
Less than 20	Self-sacrificing
20–23	Selfless
24–34	Self-aware
35–40	Self-absorbed
More than 40	Self-grandiose

WHAT DOES YOUR SCORE MEAN?

Score of 10 to 23—Heart of Gold

You wear empathy as a badge of honor. You are a kind, caring, deeply nurturing person who always has time for others. When someone needs an ear to bend or a shoulder to cry on, that person looks for you. You're a team player with a heart of gold. People count on your support, reassurance, and help with their problems. You are a great friend. However, be aware that at times others may take advantage of your compassion. Realize that sometimes it is better to put yourself first. If you find that you are being stepped on, overlooked, or just plain ignored, it is time to put yourself first. To do this, emulate someone you admire who is slightly more focused on their own interests. Practice saying "no."

Score of 24 to 40—The Golden Ruler

Your narcissistic tendencies are about average. You have a healthy balance between being selfish and selfless. You make time for others, but still keep time for you. These qualities make you a good friend. The adage "charity begins at home" suits your personality. While you work well with others in a team setting, you take pride when your own contributions are recognized. You sympathize with the plight of others and offer helpful advice, but you also remember to be careful and stay the course to your own goals and objectives.

Score of Greater than 40—Fool's Gold

You can't be bothered to listen to other people's sob stories, and frankly, you wish they'd keep their trivial problems to themselves. In fact, it is difficult for you to fully empathize with and comprehend the feelings and beliefs of others. You believe team settings allow weak-minded individuals to hide their incompetence while taking credit for your ideas and innovations. You are too important, and life is too short to waste your time dealing with people who aren't in a position to help you get ahead. You tend to have an over-inflated sense of your own importance. The higher your score, the more you share these attitudes.

Recognize that you can't help yourself if you *only* help yourself. People will see through you. Yes, first impressions are important, but lasting impressions are what matters. For you to walk a mile in another person's shoes, you may need to take small steps. Volunteer your services—without taking credit. Donate to a charity—anonymously. Try to see a concern from someone's point of view where you have no stake in the outcome.

If you scored 40 or more, you may not realize this, but your friends and colleagues will respect you more if you stop being envious of others and give them credit for their efforts. You do not need to embellish your success to be admired. Share the recognition more, and you will be better liked. People respond to generosity of wealth and spirit.

Sticks and Stones

EVALUATING YOUR NEGATIVE LABELS

While narcissists give themselves too much credit, others are their own worst critics. It may be said that sticks and stones can break our bones, but names will never hurt us—but that ain't true.

If Bobby tells himself that he is stupid, he is likely to quit participating at school—after all he would have failed the assignment anyway. If Betty believes she truly is ugly, she will forgo the makeup, wear her torn, baggy sweat suit, and decide that styling her hair is a waste of time. This is called a self-fulfilling prophecy. If you see yourself as a lost cause, you'll lose any hope for self-improvement. In the immortal words of Walt Kelly's Pogo, "We have met the enemy . . . and he is us."

TEST YOURSELF

Instructions

This next test is different from all others in this book, as it is merely a list of words. All you need to do is circle a number next to the label to indicate whether you are almost never, occasionally, or almost always this way. Remember, this is your opinion of yourself—not what you think others may feel about you. It only takes about five minutes, but there is no time limit. If you can't decide between two categories, go with your first instinct.

WARNING: Before you begin, prepare yourself for distress. You are about to read forty hurtful words. This test bothers sensitive people.

ARE YOU TOO NEGATIVE?

Circle the number which best represents your opinion:

Label	Almost Never	Occasionally	Almost Always
1. Aggressive	1	2	3
2. Bossy	1	2	3
3. Chauvinist	1	2	3
4. Cold	1	2	3
5. Competitive	1	2	3
6. Compulsive	1	2	3
7. Conceited	1	2	3
8. Critical	1	2	3
9. Demanding	1	2	3
10. Disgusting	1	2	3
11. Dull	1	2	3
12. Emotional	1	2	3
13. Failure	1	2	3
14. Hostile	1	2	3
15. Illogical	1	2	3
16. Immature	1	2	3
17. Impolite	1	2	3
18. Insensitive	1	2	3
19. Irresponsible	1	2	3
20. Klutz	1	2	3
21. Lazy	1	2	3

Label	Almost Never	Occasionally	Almost Always
22. Mean	1	2	3
23. Nagging	1	2	3
24. Nosy	1	2	3
25. Overactive	1	2	3
26. Passive	1	2	3
27. Petty	1	2	3
28. Self-pitying	1	2	3
29. Selfish	1	2	3
30. Silly	1	2	3
31. Stubborn	1	2	3
32. Stuck-up	1	2	3
33. Stupid	1	2	3
34. Too idealistic	1	2	3
35. Troublemaker	1	2	3
36. Ugly	1	2	3
37. Ungrateful	1	2	3
38. UnImportant	1	2	3
39. Weak	1	2	3
40. Wrong	1	2	3

Adapted from Peurifoy R. (1988), A List of Common Negative Labels. Used by permission.

Scoring Your Test

To find your score, add the forty numbers you circled and write on the line below.

Your Score: _____

WHAT DOES YOUR SCORE MEAN?

Score of 100 to 120—Bitter Days!

Mirror, mirror on the wall, who's the most worthless one of all? Although you believe the magic mirror is calling out your name, it isn't. Like those who go through life wearing rose-colored glasses, you see life through a negative filter. Happy, positive events are blocked from entering your mind, but the disheartening ones rush right in. Life really isn't as hopeless as you make it out to be. Bad days and mood swings are all part of the human experience. If you find yourself having too much *down* time, speak with others to learn why. Understanding that removing the filter is the first step to a brighter outlook. Additionally, don't let a single negative event turn into a pattern of self-criticism, instead think of the positive elements of your life to block the cycle. Everyone has at least a few good qualities, so focus on the things you do well.

Score of 60 to 99—Better Days!

To indicate the true meaning of your score, look them over and see if you marked mainly 1s and 3s or if you marked mostly 2s. If you are in the first category, your life is probably an emotional rollercoaster with stratospheric highs and subterranean lows. You might be a "Jekyll and Hyde" in your relationships, or you may be overly sensitive to your own moods. Chances are you are too critical of yourself. Pinpoint things that bring you down and examine them. Realize while everyone has ups and downs, you may need to try and keep your day-to-day emotions on a more even keel.

If your score is mainly 2s, you may have days where you prefer to stay in bed, but most of the time you greet the day with a smile. You tend to look at life and others with optimism. You can acknowledge your weaknesses, but usually focus on your strengths.

Score of 40 to 59—Beautiful Days!

You are the life of the party, a bon vivant who enjoys good friends and good times. Live and let live. Let the good times roll! You see the best in everyone, especially yourself. You represent the gold standard in interpersonal dynamics and know how to make friends and influence people. Of course, that's one explanation for your remarkably high score. If that radiant description seems to clash with your day-to-day reality, refer back to the earlier section on narcissism. Because sometimes, when your opinion of yourself is too high, you learn that it's a lonely opinion at the top.

Shyness and Social Inhibition

Okay, we are getting to know you a little better. We have seen how much you love yourself and how much you loathe yourself. The rest of the tests in this book cover more telling issues. We will discover odd habits and quirks in the most basic aspects of human life: eating, sleeping, fears, relationships, and sex. Now, you may be a little shy about sharing some of those thoughts. So before we move on to the more complex area of behavior, we will finish this introduction of getting to know you by revealing your shy side.

As with most things, a little shyness is good. Someone who does not possess any shyness is apt to stumble blindly into all sorts of social mishaps. Shyness should be that soft voice that cautions us to go slowly so we don't make fools of ourselves. However, shyness can be a problem when that soft voice no longer counsels caution but instead urges halt, thus paralyzing us from activities that should bring enjoyment.

We can all sympathize with the wallflower at a party who tries to blend in to the surroundings or the students who sit in the back of the classroom, slumped down in their chair to avoid the instructor's attention. You probably know someone who has confessed to a shy bladder in public restrooms. Fear of public speaking is the most common phobia—well ahead of the fear of death. Social anxiety is the third most common psychological disorder, just behind depression and alcoholism. It affects more women than men (although men are more likely to seek treatment), and usually begins in mid-adolescence. While no one wants to appear foolish, social inhibition can become a self-fulfilling prophecy, especially if there is time for the anxiety to build.

Think about Carissa. She has to give a presentation next week. Carissa knows it will go badly, and she will be embarrassed—again. Just the thought of delivering her presentation causes a cold sweat to break out on her brow, her heart to race, and her petite body to tremble. Carissa's fear is amplified because last time she had to do this she stuttered, stammered, and her mind went blank, even though she desperately tried to think of what she was supposed to say. Her friends told her to picture the audience in their underwear, the very idea made her uneasy. During her moment in the spotlight, Carissa felt faint and thought she was going to pass out. She is just too shy to perform well.

There is a vast array of shyness. The next test will indicate the magnitude of your shyness.

TEST YOURSELF

Instructions

On one hand, with only thirteen questions, this test is a breeze. On the other hand, for many, this test will be very difficult because it asks them to consider a part of their personality that they find awkward. There are no right or wrong answers and it only takes about ten minutes to complete. Regardless of where you land on the shyness scale, give each question honest thought, as your answers will give you greater insight into yourself.

HOW SHY ARE YOU?

Read each item carefully and decide to what extent it is characteristic of your feelings or behavior. Circle the number that best corresponds to your answer:

	Strongly Disagree	Disagree	Neutral	Agree	Strongly Agree
1. I feel tense when I'm with people I don't know well.	1	2	3	4	5
2. I am socially somewhat awkward.	1	2	3	4	5
3. I do *not* find it difficult to ask other people for information.	1	2	3	4	5
4. I am often uncomfortable at parties and other social functions.	1	2	3	4	5
5. When in a group of people, I have trouble thinking of the right things to talk about.	1	2	3	4	5
6. It does *not* take me long to overcome my shyness in new situations.	1	2	3	4	5
7. It is hard for me to act natural when I am meeting with new people.	1	2	3	4	5
8. I feel nervous when speaking to someone in authority.	1	2	3	4	5
9. I have *no* doubts about my social competence.	1	2	3	4	5
10. I have trouble looking someone right in the eye.	1	2	3	4	5

	Strongly Disagree	Disagree	Neutral	Agree	Strongly Agree
11. I feel inhibited in social situations.	1	2	3	4	5
12. I do *not* find it hard to talk to strangers.	1	2	3	4	5
13. I am more shy with members of the opposite sex.	1	2	3	4	5

Cheek, Jonathan M. (1983). The Revised Cheek and Buss Shyness Scale Used by permission.

Scoring Your Test

To find your score simply add the thirteen numbers you circled and write your score on the line below.

Your Score _____

UNDERSTANDING YOUR SCORE

Your Score	Percentile	Level of Shyness
13–20	15	Brazen
21–30	30	Bold
31–40	50	Balanced
41–50	70	Bashful
51–65	85	Backward

WHAT DOES YOUR SCORE MEAN?

Are you backward or brazen? The numbers will help you understand where you fall on the shyness scale. Of a large group of college students who took this test, the average score was 33.

Fifty percent of the students who took this test scored between 31 and 40. That is a fairly tight range.

Score of 13 to 20—The Bold, the Brazen, and the Beautiful

You may be blossoming, but no one will ever tag you as a wall-flower! In fact, you're the life of the party. If no one is on the dance floor, you're the one to take charge, drag others out, and insist that they have a good time. You are friendly and outgoing with strangers. You readily share personal details. It is people like you who chat about their sexual history, rant about the government, and comment on your body parts while others get nervous saying "Hi." You are likely an effective public speaker.

Of course the downside of your uninhibited, gregarious nature is the chance you might do something truly wild like skinny-dipping at the company picnic. You can be a little intimidating at times, especially to more shy, reserved individuals.

Score of 21 to 40—Pleasantly (and Often Wisely) Balanced

Your score indicates you are doing a great job balancing social caution with sociability. The likelihood is that you use the evolutionary benefit of shyness to its full advantage. You do not lead the charge onto the dance floor, but you are happy to participate and thoroughly enjoy doing so. You have learned the secret of successful relationships is both parties contributing equally. Conversations with you are fun, as you both contribute and encourage others to participate as well. People tend to like you when they get to know you.

The downside is that sometimes you are not seen as a real leader. Perhaps you are not confident enough to "seize the day," and as a consequence, lose some promising opportunities. You will not boldly stride right over to that sexy someone at a party—even though they might have been overjoyed by your zeal. By the same token, your reluctance to "dive in" with your more brazen skinny-dipping friend earns you the respect of your colleagues.

Score of 41 to 65—A Bashful, Little Wallflower

"Bashful" may be giving you too much credit. You withdraw in social situations. You get tongue-tied when asked your opinion, and you become undone in any conversation with members of the opposite sex. There are, however, upsides to this degree of shyness. You will *never* be convinced to join in the office picnic skinny-dipping team—saving yourself embarrassment, a career disaster, and a cold. The downside is that you will rarely avail yourself of the joys of social interaction and be stymied in your desire to develop meaningful relationships. After all, you struggle to present yourself to others, so getting to know you is a challenge.

Overcoming this level of shyness is a good deal like getting over an allergy by getting allergy shots. If you would like to be a little more open, inch forward! Figuratively and literally. Physically stand a little closer than usual to others in social settings. Ask family members to practice conversations with you. Of course it will be awkward to ask for help (that's part of the shyness!) but seeking that level of help is necessary to keep moving forward. Practice singing in the shower. Loudly. Dance in front of the mirror. Close your eyes and imagine yourself in an awkward situation. Then open them and realize that you are still fine. Do this repeatedly, with the situation becoming a bit more embarrassing each time, and soon you will be able to make that presentation with confidence.

SOCIAL ANXIETY DISORDER

If you call in sick the day of the presentation, and you avoid dinner parties altogether, your shyness is affecting your life. If your social inhibition significantly interferes with day-to-day activities, you may have reached the level of Social Anxiety Disorder. This disorder occurs in those intensely afraid of being judged by others which leads to feelings of inadequacy, embarrassment, and depression. The fear interferes with everyday activities, such as school or work. You realize the fears are irrational, yet cannot overcome them.

The following situations create stress in those with this disorder:

- Being introduced to people

- Being criticized

- Being the center of attention

- Being watched while doing something

- Meeting people in authority

- Being in social situations where strangers are present

- Making small talk at functions

Social phobias are so broad that they encompass any social setting. This disorder can be extremely debilitating—keeping the person home from school or work, and preventing friendships from forming. Physical symptoms include blushing, sweating, trembling, and difficulty talking. The following stories illustrate a couple of the more common social phobias.

Diane, a college student, suffers from ereuthophobia—the fear of blushing. Diane is nervous about her first day of classes because she knows the professors ask students to introduce themselves. The thought of sitting there, waiting to introduce herself to a group of strangers who will be staring at her, makes her anxious. Diane knows she will sound foolish, her face will turn beet-red, and her classmates will poke fun at her blushing.

Her anxiety is so overwhelming that she skips the first day of class to avoid the mere possibility of public introductions. Diane's fear affects her day-to-day life.

Russ has an intense fear of public ridicule—catagelophobia. Anxious about the meeting scheduled for the next day, Russ is having trouble sleeping. He knows these meetings involve coworkers talking about their current projects, and the thought of speaking in front of coworkers triggers his anxiety. Russ is especially nervous because his boss will be at the meeting. He is afraid that when it is his turn to speak, he will forget what he planned to say. Sure that his coworkers will ridicule him for sounding stupid, Russ' worst enemy is his fear.

Emily hates going to the bank. When she stands in line, she is afraid everyone is staring at her. She worries that people are watching her on the security cameras. Her fear intensifies when she reaches the front of the line and must speak to the teller. Though she tries to smile and sound friendly, she knows her voice is timid and scared. Because she is certain that she's making a fool of herself, her self-consciousness and anxiety rise. Emily's worries are very real, she suffers from scopophobia, the fear of being looked at.

People with social phobias may have more problems at work, are less likely to marry, and may not get educated to their fullest potential. The good news is that social phobias can be treated successfully. We'll talk more about fears in Chapter Five. For now, let's continue sliding down along the shyness slope.

AVOIDANT PERSONALITY DISORDER

While Social Anxiety Disorder is fostered by the fear of being judged by others, leading to embarrassment and depression, Avoidant Personality Disorder stems from fear of rejection. Rather than being rejected, which they are positive will happen, they remove themselves from the situation, thus missing out on life experiences, relationships with others, and professional successes.

Let's meet Matt and walk a few steps in his shoes. Matt is a low-level computer programmer. He has been with the same firm for years, but he has never received a promotion. Even after all these years of working with the same people, social situations are a nightmare. He could take some classes to advance his career, but this would mean interacting with others. Just the thought of having to talk with strangers makes him anxious and sweaty. He only has a few friends (gregarious coworkers who made an effort to know him and were pleased to discover that Matt is a delightful person.) He couldn't possibly date, as he knows that he would choose the wrong clothes, be unable to speak, and that he is not good-looking enough anyway.

Every day is maddening for Matt. He is lonely, but his fear of rejection is stifling his life. Matt is thin-skinned and easily upset. He is a chronic underachiever who finds excuses to miss meetings or situations where strangers might be present. Matt watches life pass him by and firmly believes that he is unable to do anything about it.

Relationships are difficult and meeting strangers is a source of great anxiety for avoidant sufferers. They become dependent on the few close relationships they already have. Although possessing a great desire for affection, they do not crave acceptance as much as they fear rejection.

While people with avoidant personalities want people to like them, they are afraid of the ridicule. They would rather live in their own little bubble than risk the rejection.

Now that we have completed the first few stops on the tour, you should start to have a better understanding of yourself and others. We have run the gamut of those who love themselves so much that others can't stand them, to those who loathe themselves so much that others can't know them. Perhaps a couple of the descriptions in this chapter reminded you of a friend or coworker; if so, I hope you now have a better understanding of how they see the world.

DO YOU HAVE
AVOIDANT PERSONALITY DISORDER?

According to psychiatrists, people with at least four of these seven maladaptive traits have Avoidant Personality Disorder:

1. You avoid work that has interpersonal contact because you are afraid of rejection and criticism.

2. You always worry about criticism or rejection in social situations.

3. You are reluctant to get involved with people unless you are confident they will like you.

4. You are withdrawn in intimate relationships to protect yourself from shame or ridicule.

5. When meeting new people, you are inhibited because you feel inadequate.

6. You believe you are socially inept, unappealing, or inferior.

7. You are reluctant to try new things because they may prove embarrassing.

2.

curious relationships:
loving you to death

The easiest kind of relationship for me is with ten thousand people. The hardest is with one.　**—JOAN BAEZ**

Can anything in life be more complex, infuriating, inviting, invigorating, or downright frustrating than human relationships? The time, effort, and compromise necessary to make a modest success of a single relationship makes you wonder if it is worth the bother. But then, you look into your loved one's eyes and see the sun rising and setting in them. The very air they breathe is special. But then they do something incredibly thoughtless, frustrating, or exasperating, and you're back to square one.

There are just too many factors, nuances, and subtleties to a relationship. Even the brightest and most insightful of us screw them up with remarkable frequency.

We all *need* to form intimate bonds with others, so why are they so darned difficult to establish and maintain? Casual relationships seem simple. A smile. A nod. A friendly greeting. These gestures make social interaction pleasurable. As we make friends, our interactions become more meaningful. We share opinions and experiences; and as the relationship grows, we fall in love. The stakes get higher—a lifetime of happiness hangs in the balance.

While forming relationships should be natural, it takes a lifetime of learning and experience to get it right. Most of us never completely succeed. As newborns, we are little more than a blob of needs—to be fed, changed, held, kept warm. Slowly, the months turn to years, and we integrate social and familial roles into our personalities. We learn to communicate. And as soon as we completely captivate our parents, we look beyond them for additional gratification. Grandparents. Siblings. Friends.

During adolescence, we begin to strike out beyond the confines of family and experiment with our own identities. In our efforts to become more independent, we rely on our friends for self-definition, companionship, and understanding of the world. Participating in family life becomes embarrassing. Good-bye kisses in front of school come to a halt. We move forward in awkward fits and spurts. Our emotions are raw and transparent, and our relationships are intense and volatile. We discover our sexual selves, opening a world of incredible energy and insecurity.

The years tick by quickly, and by adulthood, the intensity of adolescence is something most of us are happy to leave behind.

We gained experience in friendships and romance. We feel comfortable with ourselves, and we now look to the future for a relationship that will last a lifetime.

Finding the right person to form this relationship is no small feat. While some people become addicted to romantic love—with its obsessiveness, idealism, and sexual tensions—most of us realize that the passionate romance of a new relationship cannot be sustained over the years. Romance allows us to initiate our lifelong relationship, but it is not the quality that enables it to endure. For that, we must rely upon commitment and intimacy, with which we create a relationship that is strong enough to withstand life's trials, yet flexible enough to delight us with its surprises. Before we go any further, let's take a moment to assess your current relationship.

TEST YOURSELF

Instructions

Psychologists have been measuring romance for almost four decades now—with some success. This next quiz was designed by one of the leading researchers in romance. Dr. Ellen Berscheid and her colleagues have developed a great little test here to measure the push-pull of your romantic relationship.

The test consists of thirty-one statements about "X" where X is that mysterious someone special in your life. All you have to do is circle the number that best represents how much you agree with each statement.

ARE YOU INSECURE IN YOUR RELATIONSHIP?

In each question, the term "X" refers to your partner, spouse, boyfriend, girlfriend, etc. Circle the number that best represents how much you agree or disagree with each statement:

	Strongly Disagree	Moderately Disagree	Slightly Disagree	Slightly Agree	Moderately Agree	Strongly Agree
1. X's presence makes any activity more enjoyable.	1	2	3	4	5	6
2. X is close to my ideal person.	1	2	3	4	5	6
3. I am very lucky to be involved in a relationship with X.	1	2	3	4	5	6
4. I find myself wanting X when we're not together.	1	2	3	4	5	6
5. My relationship with X has given my life more direction and purpose.	1	2	3	4	5	6
6. I spend more time thinking about my career than I do about X.	6	5	4	3	2	1
7. I'd be extremely depressed for a long time if my relationship with X were to end.	1	2	3	4	5	6
8. If I couldn't have X, I'd easily find someone to replace X.	6	5	4	3	2	1

	Strongly Disagree	Moderately Disagree	Slightly Disagree	Slightly Agree	Moderately Agree	Strongly Agree
9. My relationship with X has made my life worthwhile.	1	2	3	4	5	6
10. I don't really need X.	6	5	4	3	2	1
11. I want X.	1	2	3	4	5	6
12. I am very dependent upon X.	1	2	3	4	5	6
13. I feel very proud to know X.	1	2	3	4	5	6
14. I want X to confide mostly in me.	1	2	3	4	5	6
15. I spend a great deal of time thinking about X.	1	2	3	4	5	6
16. I want X to tell me "I love you."	1	2	3	4	5	6
17. I feel very secure in my relationship with X.	6	5	4	3	2	1
18. X is a rather mysterious person.	1	2	3	4	5	6
19. I often wonder how much X really cares for me.	1	2	3	4	5	6
20. Sometimes, I wish I didn't care so much for X.	1	2	3	4	5	6
21. I worry that X doesn't care as much for me as I do for X.	1	2	3	4	5	6
22. I have great difficulty trying to figure out X.	1	2	3	4	5	6

	Strongly Disagree	Moderately Disagree	Slightly Disagree	Slightly Agree	Moderately Agree	Strongly Agree
23. I have imagined conversations I would have with X.	1	2	3	4	5	6
24. I try to plan out what I want to say before talking to X.	1	2	3	4	5	6
25. X pays enough attention to me.	6	5	4	3	2	1
26. I feel uneasy if X is making friends with someone of the opposite sex.	1	2	3	4	5	6
27. I need X more than X needs me.	1	2	3	4	5	6
28. X has been the cause of some of my worst depressions.	1	2	3	4	5	6
29. My relationship with X is stable and quietly satisfying.	6	5	4	3	2	1
30. There is little conflict between X and myself.	6	5	4	3	2	1
31. I worry about losing X's affection.	1	2	3	4	5	6

Berscheid, E., Attridge, M., and Sprecher, S. (1998). Dependency and Insecurity in Romantic Relationships: Development and Validation of Two Companion Scales. Personal Relationships, 5, 31–58. Used by permission.

Scoring Your Test

This clever test has two parts: dependency and insecurity. One will measure your relationship strength, the other looks for a killer.

To find your scores, simply add the numbers you circled in each of the following questions:

Your Relationship Dependency Score _____
(questions 1 to 16)

Your Relationship Insecurity Score _____
(questions 17 to 31)

Understanding Your Score

RELATIONSHIP DEPENDENCY

Your Score	Percentile	Relationship Dependency
51 or less	15	Frail
61	30	Flimsy
71	50	Firm
81	70	Fantastic
91 or more	85	Fanatical

WHAT DOES YOUR SCORE MEAN?
Dependency Score of less than 61—Like a Rolling Stone
Your relationship is somewhat fragile in that you do not necessarily look to your partner to fulfill emotional needs. You are an autonomous, free-spirited independent collaborator in your

friendship. Perhaps your relationship is newly budding, or perhaps dying on the vine, but based on your answers, you do not need your partner in the traditional sense of couplehood.

Dependency Score of 61 to 80—Loves Me Like a Rock

Doing well! You have the bonding thing going in the conventional manner. Your score is just about average for young adults in the United States. You have a healthy balance between being needy and being an independent person. Check out your insecurity score as well, as this will help sway the success of your relationship.

Dependency Score of more than 80—Solid as a Rock

Hot dog! Fairy tales do come true. You love to share your life with your partner. You get that special warm, gooey feeling whenever you think of your other half. If your security score is 30 or higher—congratulations, you have hit the romance jackpot.

RELATIONSHIP INSECURITY

Your Score	Percentile	Relationship Insecurity
17 or less	15	Tranquility
28	30	Serenity
38	50	Security
48	70	Trepidation
57 or more	85	Anxiety

Insecurity Score of less than 28—Warm and Fuzzy

Great job! You have a very healthy level of security. Your relationship is one of trust and respect. You are probably married or in a long-term, exclusive relationship. You don't spend time worrying about your partner's devotion, as you both enjoy the warm, fuzzy blanket of a committed relationship.

Insecurity Score of 28 to 48—Shared Warmth
Very good. Your feelings of security are about average for younger American couples. At times you wonder about your love, but your romance tends to stay on track. The success of your relationship will also depend greatly on your dependency score. For example, if you got a high dependency score, you and your partner need each other to share this warmth. However, a low dependency score indicates your level of commitment might leave you cold.

Insecurity Score of Over 48—Left Out in the Cold?
Your relationship is in trouble. You spend far too much time worrying whether your partner truly cares for you. Begin an open dialogue, get these issues discussed out in the open. Have your partner take this test. If both of you score high on the dependent sections, your relationship has potential, you just need more assurance of love. If your dependency scores are low, your relationship may be based on factors like physical attractiveness, sex, and convenience. If you both want this relationship to work, roll up your sleeves, as it is going to take an effort.

Now we've seen the importance of reliance and security. Why is it that strong relationships elude so many of us? What is it that makes successful, long-term relationships so difficult? Let's visit some relationship killers . . .

Relationship Killers

Relationships are the threads that weave us into the fabric of society. Generally, the tapestry is bold and powerful. However, individual threads can be weak and tenuous. The following are some of the things we do to tear, tug, and torment those threads, and limit our ability to enter into satisfying relationships.

JEALOUSY

When some people hear the word "jealousy," they immediately visualize some hotheaded, irrational behavior. For example, take the man whose wife answers the door in her robe and smiles as she thanks the deliveryman. The husband, witnessing this scene, deems the robe is open a little too far, immediately assumes the two are having an affair. He jumps up from the couch and berates the deliveryman. Extreme jealousy is certainly a relationship killer, but not all jealousy is bad. In fact, we are hardwired to be jealous.

While it is true that people are not possessions, the sense of intimacy we feel toward loved ones is the cement that allows us to trust and build foundations for the future. Healthy jealousy is the emotion that motivates us to protect our relationships, to appreciate and strengthen our bonds. It makes us care. However,

Extreme jealousy is a relationship killer.

when jealousy becomes excessive, it can erode those bonds, shatter the trust, and destroy a relationship.

The question is not whether you're jealous, but rather, how healthy is your jealousy. Let's see . . .

TEST YOURSELF

Instructions

There are twenty-five situations described in this test. WARNING: This test contains some upsetting situations that might awaken the green-eyed monster. Imagine yourself in each situation. Consider how you would truly feel. Circle the number that best represents your emotions. There are no right or wrong answers. Be honest, this is an opportunity to learn about yourself and your relationship. The test should take you about ten minutes, but feel free to take longer. There are no time limits.

HOW JEALOUS ARE YOU?

Indicate how you would feel if you were confronted with the situations listed below by circling the number that best corresponds to your emotions:

	Pleased	Mildly Upset	Upset	Very Upset	Extremely Upset
1. Your partner expresses the desire that you both develop other romantic relationships.	1	2	3	4	5
2. Your partner spends increasingly more time at work with a fellow employee you feel could be sexually attractive to your partner.	1	2	3	4	5
3. Your partner suddenly shows an interest in going to a party when he or she finds out that someone will be there with whom he or she has been romantically involved previously.	1	2	3	4	5
4. At a party, your partner hugs someone other than you.	1	2	3	4	5
5. You notice your partner repeatedly looking at another person.	1	2	3	4	5
6. Your partner spends increasingly more time in outside activities and hobbies in which you are not interested.	1	2	3	4	5
7. At a party, your partner kisses someone you do not know.	1	2	3	4	5

	Pleased	Mildly Upset	Upset	Very Upset	Extremely Upset
8. Your boss, with whom you had a good working relationship in the past, now seems to be more interested in the work of a coworker.	1	2	3	4	5
9. Your partner goes to a bar several evenings without you.	1	2	3	4	5
10. Your partner recently received a promotion, and the new position requires a great deal of travel, business dinners, and parties, most of which you are not invited to attend.	1	2	3	4	5
11. At a party, your partner dances with someone you do not know.	1	2	3	4	5
12. You and a coworker worked very hard on an extremely important project. However, your boss gave your coworker full credit for it.	1	2	3	4	5
13. Someone flirts with your partner.	1	2	3	4	5
14. At a party, your partner repeatedly kisses someone you do not know.	1	2	3	4	5
15. Your partner has sexual relations with someone else.	1	2	3	4	5
16. Your brother or sister was given more freedom, such as staying up later or driving the car.	1	2	3	4	5
17. Your partner comments to you how attractive another person is.	1	2	3	4	5

	Pleased	Mildly Upset	Upset	Very Upset	Extremely Upset
18. While at a social gathering of a group of friends, your partner spends little time talking to you, but engages the others in animated conversation.	1	2	3	4	5
19. Grandparents visit your family, and they seem to devote most of the attention to a brother or sister instead of you.	1	2	3	4	5
20. Your partner flirts with someone else.	1	2	3	4	5
21. Your brother or sister seems to be receiving more affection and/or attention from your parents.	1	2	3	4	5
22. You have just discovered your partner is having an affair with someone at work.	1	2	3	4	5
23. The person who has been your assistant for a number of years at work decides to take a similar position with some other company.	1	2	3	4	5
24. The group to which you belong appears to be leaving you out of plans, activities, etc.	1	2	3	4	5
25. Your best friend suddenly shows interest in doing things with someone else.	1	2	3	4	5

Bringle, R. G., Roach, S., Andler, C., and Evenbeck, S. (1979). Measuring the Intensity of Jealous Reactions. Catalog of Selected Documents in Psychology, 9 23–24. Used by permission.

Scoring Your Test

To score your test, simply add the twenty-five numbers you circled and write your score on the line below.

Your score _____

If you are in a long-term relationship, you might find it useful to compare your answers to your partner's.

Your Score	Percentile	Level of Jealousy
25–35	15	Happy, Sunny Yellow
36–50	30	Relaxed, Tranquil Blue
51–75	50	Neutral Beige
76–95	70	Seething Green-Eyed Monster
96–125	85	Raging, Raving Red

WHAT DOES YOUR SCORE MEAN?

Score of 25 to 50—Chillin', whatever

You are a bona-fide member of the bottom third of the population with the physiological anomaly of not having a jealous bone in your body. You are confident in your relationship. You trust your partner without question. This can make you a wonderful spouse. It also means that you are just as likely to allow the love of your life to leave you without any fight. You have such faith in your relationship that your partner may have trouble knowing if you are totally trusting or you simply don't care. This may cause your mate to test your love.

Score of 51 to 75—Trusting, but Wary

If you scored in this range, you are average in your jealousy rating. You are part of the great middle of people who are situationally jealous. That is, the same thing that unnerves you in one context might not bother you in another. A particular behavior that troubles you at the end of a busy day will not even rate on your scale after a weekend of hand-holding on the beach. You generally have a healthy level of protectiveness of your mate. Sometimes, you look into your partner's eyes and know they are yours forever. Other times . . . well, they are keeping you just enough off balance to ensure you're going to bring flowers.

Score of 76 to 125—Get the Fire Hose Ready!

Being with someone who scores in this range is like wearing a red blouse in front of an angry bull. In this relationship, you are constantly on guard. You are fearful of any behavior that might be misconstrued and enrage the bull. You become reluctant to grow as an individual—one of the most important aspects of a relationship—and you often allow relationships with family or friends to simply wither away.

Those who score in the top third for jealousy know the green-eyed monster on a first-name basis. You require candid communication to appease your suspicious nature. It is the only way to tame the beast. Reassurance is vital, but it should not be artificially flattering. The problem lies not in your partner's behavior, but in your perceptions and reactions to your partner. You must learn to trust.

If you are in a relationship with someone who got a high score, the best tactic is to take the bull by the horns and communicate frankly and frequently. Explain how the jealousy makes you feel and what you want your partner to do in the future. Have a signal to make your companion realize that jealousy is rearing its ugly head. Reassure your mate that you want your relationship to succeed.

Machiavellianism

Now we have learned a little about you and your feelings of love, insecurity, and jealousy. We are going to take the tour to a slightly darker area of your mind . . .

Do nice guys finish last? Does the end justify the means? Is success—no matter what it takes—your motto? If you answered yes, then you have Machiavellian tendencies. Nicolo Machiavelli was a government worker who spent his life observing the traits of leaders. In his book, *The Prince,* Machiavelli wrote that princes should retain control of their territories using any means necessary—including deceit—and should be relentless in doing so. His name has become synonymous with users and manipulators who do anything to get what they want.

So, if you lie, cheat, and steal to get what you want, is that success? If you build a long-term, tender, caring relationship, but have to compromise on key desires, is that failure? We can build relationships through deceit or compromise. Few of us choose one path or the other, we reacted situationally. Sometimes we share and cooperate, at other times we force our will on others. Let's see how your personality scores . . .

TEST YOURSELF

Instructions

The following questionnaire allows you to evaluate your self-ishness and sharing tendencies. It will help you determine how they affect your relationships. The questionnaire consists of only twenty questions and should not take more than ten minutes to complete, but there is no time limit. Mark your answers on the page by circling the number that best represents your opinion.

Indicate below the extent to which you agree or disagree with each of the following:

	Strongly Disagree	Disagree	Neutral	Agree	Strongly Agree
1. The best way to handle people is to tell them what they want to hear.	1	2	3	4	5
2. When you ask someone to do something for you, it is best to give the real reasons for wanting it rather than giving reasons that might carry more weight.	5	4	3	2	1
3. Anyone who completely trusts anyone else is asking for trouble.	1	2	3	4	5
4. It is hard to get ahead without cutting corners here and there.	1	2	3	4	5
5. Honesty is the best policy in all cases.	5	4	3	2	1
6. It is safest to assume that all people have a vicious streak, and it will come out when given a chance.	1	2	3	4	5
7. Never tell anyone the real reason you did something unless it is useful to do so.	1	2	3	4	5
8. One should take action only when sure it is morally right.	5	4	3	2	1
9. It is wise to flatter important people.	1	2	3	4	5

	Strongly Disagree	Disagree	Neutral	Agree	Strongly Agree
10. All in all, it is better to be humble and honest than important and dishonest.	5	4	3	2	1
11. Barnum was very wrong when he said there's a sucker born every minute.	5	4	3	2	1
12. People suffering from incurable diseases should have the choice of being put painlessly to death.	1	2	3	4	5
13. It is possible to be good in all respects.	5	4	3	2	1
14. Most people are basically good and kind.	5	4	3	2	1
15. There is no excuse for lying to someone else.	5	4	3	2	1
16. Most men forget more easily the death of their father than the loss of their property.	1	2	3	4	5
17. Most people who get ahead in the world lead clean, moral lives.	5	4	3	2	1
18. Generally speaking, men won't work hard unless they're forced to do so.	1	2	3	4	5
19. The biggest difference between most criminals and other people is that criminals are stupid enough to get caught.	1	2	3	4	5
20. Most men are brave.	5	4	3	2	1

Reprinted from Christie, R. and Geis, F.L. (1970). Studies in Machiavellianism. New York: Elsevier.

Scoring Your Test

To find your score, simply add the numbers you've circled and write your answer on the line below.

Your Score _____

UNDERSTANDING YOUR SCORE

Your Score	Your Personality
20–40	Caring
41–50	Considerate
51–70	Capable
71–80	Controlling
81–100	Cutthroat

WHAT DOES YOUR SCORE MEAN?

Score of 20 to 50—Pussycat!

If you scored in this range, you are a kindhearted idealist who looks for the best in everyone you meet. You have strong opinions of what is right and wrong, which sometimes cause conflict with others. More likely, you are a pushover and allow yourself to be manipulated much too easily. You tend to let people and events determine your options and decisions. Very low scorers tend to be dependent and submissive. Be wary of those who score above 70 on this test—they will try to play you like a cheap fiddle.

Score of 51 to 70—A Diplomat!

You are someone who shares the remote while still standing up for the programs you want to watch. You occupy a fairly balanced place on this scale. Not too wimpy, and yet not too demanding. You tend to be a little cautious about trusting human nature, yet are idealistic at times. For you, the selfishness of others is an annoyance, as it spoils your admirable vision of society. You are most likely to negotiate healthy solutions and outcomes that are satisfying to everyone involved. And you realize that compromise is not capitulation.

Score of 71 to 100—Determined Manipulator

If you scored between 71 and 100, you are unwilling to let anything stand in the way of your needs and wants. You require to rule your roost. Obstacles in your path are annoyances, and you will resort to any play—moral or otherwise—to obliterate them. You can be charming, confident, and glib, but you are also seen as arrogant, calculating, and cynical. Using deceit to manipulate others is just one part of your playbook. Unfortunately, unless you find a partner who scored low on the test, your relationship is likely to be characterized by constant strife and subterfuge.

Lies and the Lying Liars Who Tell Them

Deceit is an easily accessible tool of the Machiavellian personality, and with our culture rewarding the "I want, I need" mentality of fellow citizens, it is worth exploring how lies and lying can affect relationships—for good and for bad.

WHITE LIES

People who enter into relationships wanting and expecting total honesty have read way too many fairy tales. The world is a messy place. It is a difficult place to negotiate. There are major cultural traditions that not only acknowledge the existence of "white lies," but demand the use of them. For example, your wife/girlfriend has just purchased a new dress that she is thrilled

Sometimes there is no harm in telling a little white lie.

about. She models it for you. Only a fool would suggest that she looks a little hefty in it. Instead we smile and reply, "That's lovely on you." Are you telling the absolute truth? No. But you are shaping the truth to spare their feelings and aid the success of your relationship. Nothing is wrong with that.

Think of leaders who take the podium and give all the credit to their subordinates. We admire and respect them for that. We value humility. Yet, humility is a white lie. It denies the truth. If the leaders were telling the absolute truth, they would take at least some of the credit, but a little white lie enhances the relationship with coworkers.

DARK LIES

By definition, "dark lies" are the opposite of white lies. Their purpose is more sinister and self-serving. A white lie elevates a partner's feelings. It is altruistic. A dark lie is selfish. It exaggerates accomplishments and diminishes others. Telling someone that a dress looks lovely on them is vastly different than *not* telling someone about a major indiscretion that you committed. While white lies seek the betterment of a relationship; dark lies gnaw at the trusting bond and can ultimately destroy it.

PATHOLOGICAL LIARS

When you think of a pathological liar, you likely think of someone who makes outlandish, dramatic claims—"I am a surgeon and I fly helicopters for the Navy SEALs," or something equally preposterous. Pathological liars portray themselves as braver, smarter, and more attractive than they really are. If you hear a twenty-five-year-old describing in brilliant detail his wartime heroics in Vietnam, you know you are listening to a pathological liar.

Although they make peculiar claims that others know are untrue, the pathological liar cannot seem not to lie. One fascinating aspect of these people is that they believe the lie while they are telling it. To them, the stories are true. The lies are impulsive, there is no planning. The pathological liar lies about meaningless things. They lie about what they ate for breakfast. They lie about who they were talking on the phone with. They lie about what color tie they are wearing. And the most pitiful aspect of their lying is how easily such things are found out. Generally, the only purpose for the lies is to elevate themselves and impress others.

Pathological liars cover up their lies with still more lies—and then more lies. They become trapped within their stories. Being in a relationship with a pathological liar is like trying to swim against the ocean current a hurricane. It is exhausting and impossible to reach calm serene water.

Down in the Dumps

There is a secret enemy killing many marriages in the United States—that slow assassin is depression. Depression erodes and destroys the strongest of relationships bit by bit. When men are asked what they most want from their marriage, they tend to say "to make my wife happy." It is a simple, lovely goal that gives both spouses satisfaction. Depression poisons this dynamic. Once a woman becomes a depression victim, she can no longer express her appreciation and love for her partner. The partner, in turn, feels like a failure for being unable to fulfill his goal. Frequently, those afflicted with depression have no idea why they have lost interest in the joys of life. According to the National Institute of Mental Health, almost 10 percent of Americans will suffer with a depressive disorder this year. Women are twice as likely as men to be diagnosed. Without a doubt, you know someone with depression. I was exceptionally happily married to my high school sweetheart for seventeen years until depression crept in and took her from me. Do yourself a favor, learn about this disease before it ruins another relationship.

GRUMPY OLD MAN SYNDROME

One common but relatively unknown type of depression is the Grumpy Old Man Syndrome. You've seen them, the grumpy old men. Couch potatoes. The sneer on their faces where happy smiles once resided. The man who used to hop up from his chair at any chance to play catch with his son, now can't be bothered to do much of anything. The man with a zest for life who used to wake up each morning with an erection is now mired in misery.

DO YOU HAVE DEPRESSION?

Depression is rampant in the United States. As many as 20 percent of women and 10 percent of men will suffer from this condition in their lifetime. Right now, over 10 million Americans are afflicted with a major depressive disorder.

If you answer yes to at least five of the following, seek professional help immediately.

For the last two weeks or more have you . . .

Been sad, tearful, or feeling blue? YES NO

Lost interest or pleasure in activities you once enjoyed? YES NO

Found an increase or decrease in your appetite and have lost or gained weight? YES NO

Had trouble sleeping or found you sleep too much? YES NO

Felt tired, like you have no energy? YES NO

Felt worthless or guilty or regretful about things you've done or things you have not done? YES NO

Had trouble making decisions, concentrating, or thinking things through? YES NO

Had thoughts about killing yourself or felt that you would be better off dead? YES NO

Been bothered by these symptoms enough to cause you distress, impair your relationships, or affect your employment? YES NO

"Why bother?" he mutters. Grumpy Old Man Syndrome has a veritable shopping list of symptoms:

- Reduced sex drive

- Erectile dysfunction

- Depression

- Disturbed sleep

- Prostate enlargement

- Low energy

- Muscle weakness

- General miserableness

We are beginning to understand that body chemistry changes explain why their get up and go has got up and gone. Medical researchers are beginning to recognize this syndrome as andropause,

the male equivalent to menopause, which is marked by the decrease in the body's production of testosterone.

Soon it may be possible to renew your old man's vim and vigor, but in the meantime, recognize that he is not miserable by choice.

Killer Relationships

While there are numerous personality traits that kill a relationship, there are still other relationships that rely on destructive traits to attempt to *strengthen* the bonds of the relationship.

MUNCHAUSEN'S SYNDROME

From the infant suckling at his mother's breast to the confused adolescent, all children crave the nurturing attention of their parents. Is there a more innocent pleasure than being cuddled and cared for by someone who loves you beyond measure? Our boundless love as parents leads us to shower our sick children with even more attention than usual. And herein lays the seeds of Munchausen's (pronounced "MUN-chow-zens") Syndrome.

Children are intelligent and inquisitive creatures. They understand simple cause-and-effect dynamics, and it doesn't take them long to figure out how to manipulate their situations. Take, for example, my own son. When he was eighteen months old, he developed a nasty cough. For three days, my wife and I hovered over him, showering him with our worried love and affection. Even after the doctor pronounced his lungs clear, his cough lingered in a strange way and had the curious quality of growing worse when he found himself alone. While we played with him, fed him, interacted with him there was no cough. But after a few minutes of playing by himself, it would return! It was only when I mentioned this observation to my wife that she realized it too. "And he has this little smile when we come scurrying over . . ."

she added as it dawned on both of us exactly what was happening. Our sweet bundle of joy had played us! Our innocent little boy had discovered the power of Munchausen's Syndrome.

Munchausen's Syndrome is a medical condition characterized by faking health problems in order to get attention. It is named after Karl Friedrich Hieronymous von Munchausen, who, in order to make his life sound a little more exciting, embellished his tales of war, hunting, and travel. The Baron's stories became so widely told that the von Munchausen name became synonymous with outlandish tales. In 1951, the psychiatric community drew on the name in identifying a syndrome where people feign illness when they are not ill. People who suffer from Munchausen's *are* sick, just not from the various illnesses they fake. For unexplained reasons, women suffer more frequently from this condition, but the men who suffer from it tend to behave in a more dramatic and severe fashion.

In order for a diagnosis of Munchausen to be made, a patient must:

a) Deliberately fake either physical or psychological symptoms and

b) Be motivated by their desire to be viewed sympathetically as a legitimate patient.

People suffering from Munchausen's do not fake these symptoms in order to collect insurance money, receive prescription drugs, avoid work, or improve their health. They seek only attention. They are like contortionists, willing to twist themselves in all sorts of impossible poses for the attention.

While my eighteen-month-old son was limited in his ability to use illness to gain attention, adults with Munchausen's Syndrome go to extraordinary lengths to gain attention. The more common ploys involve secretly swallowing blood and then re-gurgitating it in an emergency room, stabbing a finger and letting it bleed into a urine sample, or injecting their skin with feces or an irritating chemical.

This is not hypochondria, a condition in which people visit many physicians believing that they are sick. In Munchausen's Syndrome, patients know the illness they present does not exist, but choose to create an illusion of illness in order to gain attention.

Munchausen by Proxy

Ever hear the expression, "You only hurt the one you love"? You probably thought of it as a line on a Hallmark card. Most of us do not intentionally hurt—physically or emotionally—the ones we love. However, that is not the case with those suffering from Munchausen by Proxy.

Marcia, a doting mother of four, is sitting on a hard plastic chair in an emergency room. The fluorescent lights seem to high-light her worry as she holds her six-year-old, Jordan, in her lap. Poor little Jordan. She always seems to be the one to get sick or hurt. Thankfully, Marcia seems to have boundless love to show

---

A FAKING RECORD

According to the 1993 *Guinness Book of Records*, William McIl-hoy earned the record for faking medical illness. Over the course of fifty years, he had cost Britain's National Hospital Service more than $4 million.

"He had 400 major and minor operations in 100 different hos-pitals under 22 aliases. After a stay in a hospital for six months in 1979, he became weary of hospitals and hung up his bedpan to go to a retirement home, where he died in 1983."

---

her little girl, helping her through her bouts with allergic reactions, coughs, and eczema. The poor thing! She has missed so much school that the principal is considering holding her back a grade.

You have to hand it to Marcia, though. What a mom! Long-suffering. Devoted. Caring. She never complains about the trials and tribulations of having a child like Jordan. Never wavers in her patience and love. Why, Marcia even had to leave her job in order to take care of her daughter. It seems her life is spent ferrying Jordan from one doctor or clinic to the next. Her husband isn't much help. He's either too busy with work or just not around. Marcia has no choice. Little Jordan needs her mother.

Caring for Jordan has become Marcia's vocation. Not only does she shower her little girl with love and affection, but she also spends time on the Internet researching her many symptoms. She is conversant with the current medical terminology and treatment options. She recalls the patterns of her daughter's illnesses that would put a nurse to shame.

At the doctor's office, clinic, or hospital, Marcia is clearly in control. She is armed with knowledge and a mother's determination to make sure her daughter is well treated. And while Marcia is concerned about Jordan's condition, she enjoys her role. Nothing makes her happier than to spend several minutes talking about Jordan. The local paper even ran a short article about poor Jordan's ailments. As a result, Marcia has become something of a local celebrity. "Devoted Mom." That's Marcia.

After fourteen months, Jordan's various doctors began to see a pattern. Someone noted that Jordan seemed to come in almost exclusively on weekends or in the evenings. "It's as if being at school makes her better," one of the nurses mused. And just like that, all the pieces fell into place.

Jordan was certainly ill. She suffered from a condition known as Munchausen by Proxy. This is a bizarre variation of Munchausen's Syndrome in which a child is used as a surrogate. Marcia was making Jordan sick. In this strange condition, the parent—almost always the mother—will sabotage blood and urine samples. She will even injure the child by inducing vomiting, diarrhea, respiratory arrest (by smothering!), bleeding, infections, rashes, and by creating a general failure to thrive. The children not only suffer from the parents' actions, but are subjected to an extensive array of invasive radiological, medical, and surgical procedures that are unnecessary and painful. While victims tend to be preschoolers, newborns, teens, and even adults are on record as being victimized by people with this condition.

Many require hospitalization, and nearly 10 percent die as a result of their mother's relentless sickness.

As you might suspect, any suggestion of the existence of this condition is met with righteous indignation. Mothers react with outrage when told that their most basic maternal instinct—to protect their child—is being twisted to suggest that they are Munchausen by Proxy sufferers. Many parents have mounted a concerted effort to strike any mention of Munchausen Syndrome by Proxy from medical journals since they were just "being good mothers."

Not only are these syndromes tricky to diagnose, they are even more elusive to cure. Psychiatric treatment is almost always refused or circumvented. For most sufferers of Munchausen's and its related disorders, early recognition of the disorder is the best management.

Malingering

Just the term "malingerer" has a certain sinister sound to it. It conjures up dark and shadowy images of scoundrels and ne'er-do-wells. But if you have ever faked or exaggerated an illness or injury to avoid a situation or to gain something, then you are numbered amongst the ranks of malingerers. This might be as simple as faking a headache to get out of work, school, or sex; feigning menstrual cramps to be excused from gym class; or complaining of severe pain in order to receive a prescription for narcotics. Almost all of us have malingered at some point.

Fictitious Bereavement

Meet Pam, a single 27-year-old. She's kind of cute, kind of bright, and has kind of a dark side. Pam is a secretary for a group of six statisticians I know. I used to stop by her desk every couple of months while visiting her bean-counter bosses. Pam is a friendly sort, she liked to chat, but the statisticians she served only knew numbers—nothing about people. One day while passing her station, I noticed that she had a few sympathy cards on her desk. Normally, this would not be cause for comment, but I noticed different sorry-for-your-loss cards a couple of months prior. I mentioned that I was sorry to hear of her loss and asked how close she was to the deceased. She humbly answered, but there was something . . . something impish about her response. Probably five months passed before I needed to visit her office again. You guessed it—sympathy cards.

Pam collected sympathy cards and plenty of paid time off from her bosses because she periodically told them about losing family members. A knowing look followed by a couple of questions and Pam spilled her beans. Her family was fine, her sister just had a baby. Pam malingers to receive extra vacation days (you'd be surprised how many funerals take place on Fridays.) Pam also wrestles with psychological elements of fear of failure, loneliness, and that impish quality. Her bosses remained oblivious of Pam's office trick.

Surrogate Relationships

All of the relationship killers make it difficult, but not impossible, for a person to establish a successful relationship. So, what happens to people like Pam who cannot have those essential relationships? They approximate them with surrogates.

Know anyone who speaks to her cats and cares for them like children? How about the husband who prefers sitting alone in solitude with a fishing pole to spending time with his wife? What is he finding in solitude that he cannot find in his relationship? Do you know the Wall Street mogul who is so obsessed with money, he cannot love people? People who look to religion as a surrogate for flesh-and-blood relationships? Those who lack the know-how or gumption to form bonds settle for surrogates.

Crazy Relationships

As much as humans need each other, forming relationships is tough and maintaining them is grueling. We have many strange quirks that color our personalities and they contribute to relationship difficulties. However, knowledge is power. The more you know, the more you can understand others and work toward change and acceptance. If you have a controlling partner, understanding Machiavellianism can help you improve your relationship. If the jealousy test rang some bells at home, dig deeper. Perhaps you know someone with Grumpy Old Man Syndrome? Learn about it, your insight might improve their life. Now we have gotten to know each other a little better, let's pretend that we have formed a special relationship on our tour. It's time for a date. Let's go get something to eat . . .

3.

consumed with passion:
eating and drinking disorders

There is no love sincerer, than the love of food.

—GEORGE BERNARD SHAW

Ah, at last, a juicy topic we can really sink our teeth into! While man might not live by bread alone, the fact is we certainly *enjoy* making food a vital part of our lives. Just the other day, I was with friends who were discussing what they were going to eat for dinner while they were still eating lunch! I could hardly enjoy my meal for the juicy imaginings of the next feast.

Eating, like forming relationships, is a primary need, hence it is besotted with oddities. This chapter will help you determine whether your eating habits are normal, quirky, or just plain bizarre.

But first a little background knowledge. On a physical level, when our stomach is empty, it contracts and screams to our brain, "feed me!" Blood glucose levels and fatty acids trigger the impulse to hunt down a woolly mammoth to devour. At least that's how it worked in the Stone Age when there was a primitive balance between eating and survival. Unfortunately, our appetites outgrew our physical needs, and we ended up in the deep fryer with the fries. We began to rely on routine—"noon, time to eat!"—on presentation—"say, that *looks* good!"—on comfort—"I had a terrible day, pass the ice cream!" Psychologists sort our behavior into major eating personalities. While there is a little overlap in these categories (think of them as a stew rather than separate dishes), there are subtle differences that distinguish them. While you may picture yourself in one of the categories, being part of the smorgasbord of personalities is quite normal.

The Uninhibited Eater

The Uninhibited Eater, true to her title, has no shame. When Mindy is hungry . . . well, she throws herself right into the main course, as well as the dessert table. Midnight snacks? No problem. A hot dog at the street-corner cart? Pile on the sauerkraut. An extra scoop of double Dutch chocolate? Don't forget the hot fudge and sprinkles. Make no mistake, Mindy would eat like this on a first date, second date, or in the presence of her eighth-grade social studies teacher, on whom she had an incredible crush. Mindy is a concessionaire's dream. She has no guilt nor shame. She is ruled completely by the id of her hunger.

The Oversnacker

Stan, like Mindy, feels no guilt or shame when he wants to eat. But unlike Mindy, he tends not to make a spectacle of himself. Instead of piling it on all at once, Stan will nibble all day and night. While watching television, while playing cards, while waiting for his next meal. Hunger rarely enters into Stan's eating con-

siderations. He grazes throughout the day. Sometimes, you'll find him in front of the fridge, door agape, just admiring the view.

The Binger

Being with a binger is a bit like riding a roller coaster that has a tendency to fly off the tracks. Tracey is a binger. Her entire thought process centers on food. She anticipates, plans, relishes the thought of every meal. She may go hours without eating and then watch out! She will consume vast amounts of food. Prodigious amounts. She'll eat whether she's hungry or not. She will never leave a morsel of food on her plate. She'll eat pounds of food she doesn't even like! Tracey will be filled with remorse after her binge, but she can't help it. She has an emotional connection to food that goes far beyond any healthy eating habits.

Consummate Dieter

Has Tim ever *not* been on a diet? Not to anyone's recollection. He has encyclopedic knowledge of every diet perpetrated on the public. And why not? He has tried every single one of them. He has intimate knowledge of nutritional and caloric value of every food—natural or processed. He can tell you the trans fat level in every box of cake mix on the supermarket shelves. He knows the salt content of every soup. He is a linguistic expert when it comes to all the different names that add up to "sugar." He is obsessed with charts and menu plans. Tim is a good dieter. He can close his eyes and actually picture how he will look twenty-five pounds thinner. And he does lose weight on every diet plan. But he gains it back as soon as he falls off the wagon, thus repeating the vicious cycle.

Filled to the Gills

Remember the feeling on Thanksgiving Day after you devoured that delectable turkey, stuffing, mashed potatoes, green bean casserole, and don't forget the pumpkin pie? The feeling that you can't move except to roll to the recliner where you lie comatose for the next couple hours? This is Marty after every meal. While most people conclude a meal by saying, "That was delicious." Marty is more apt to say, "If I eat another bite, I'll be sick." The likelihood is that as he's making this statement, he's stabbing whatever is left on your plate. Marty never travels with less than three different name-brand antacids in his pocket.

Super-sized and Hold the Culpability

Beverly will tell you that she is "big-boned." Or, she'll mention her thyroid condition. "My metabolism is so slow it's almost at a stop." Or, "being large runs in my family—it's hereditary." Poor Beverly. It doesn't matter what she does, she is doomed to gain weight. No amount of exercise or healthy food will change that, so why bother? She might as well eat everything she wants. After all, she is cursed by the "fat gene."

Emotional Eaters

We all connect food to special occasions—turkey at Thanksgiving, hot dogs on the Fourth of July, and eggnog for New Year's. Similarly, no family gathering is complete without Aunt Edie's secret family recipe. The problem arises when the food continually becomes a means of filling an emotional void instead of our stomachs. For example, Eliot devoured gallons of rocky road when his life was dull and unexciting. Betty ate a barnyard of chicken (all fried) when she went through a period of depression. Nothing is better than Mom's chicken noodle soup when you are under the weather. Indeed, some food *does* affect mood. There are "feel-good" chemicals in chocolate. Alcohol can loosen inhibitions. Toast can soothe an upset stomach. But if you consistently rely on food to make you feel better, it is time to take a deeper look at your life.

Do You Avoid Seeing Your Body?

Your body is more than a receptacle for food. Your body is a tool. It gets you around from place to place, it has curves and straight parts, it allows us to see, hear, and touch life, it carries our brains, it can be very sexy. The following quiz will give you some insight on how your body affects your mind and, therefore, your eating choices.

TEST YOURSELF

Instructions

One of the leading experts on psychology and the body, University of Vermont professor Dr. James Rosen, created this questionnaire in response to the pressure we get from Hollywood on having the perfect body. This test goes beyond issues such as "I don't like my body" to measure how our body image affects our behavior.

This questionnaire consists of nineteen statements. All you have to do is circle the number which best describes how frequently you act on each one.

DO YOU HATE YOUR BODY?

Circle the number which best represents how often you engage in these behaviors:

	Always	Usually	Often	Sometimes	Rarely	Never
1. I wear baggy clothes.	1	2	3	4	5	6
2. I wear clothes I do not like.	1	2	3	4	5	6
3. I wear darker color clothing.	1	2	3	4	5	6
4. I wear a special set of clothing, e.g., my "fat clothes."	1	2	3	4	5	6
5. I restrict the amount of food I eat.	1	2	3	4	5	6
6. I only eat fruits, vegetables, and other low-calorie foods.	1	2	3	4	5	6
7. I fast for a day or longer.	1	2	3	4	5	6
8. I do not go out socially if I will be "checked out."	1	2	3	4	5	6
9. I do not go out socially if the people I am with will discuss weight.	1	2	3	4	5	6
10. I do not go out socially if the people I am with are thinner than me.	1	2	3	4	5	6
11. I do not go out socially if it involves eating.	1	2	3	4	5	6

	Always	Usually	Often	Sometimes	Rarely	Never
12. I weigh myself.	1	2	3	4	5	6
13. I am inactive.	1	2	3	4	5	6
14. I look at myself in the mirror.	6	5	4	3	2	1
15. I avoid physical intimacy.	1	2	3	4	5	6
16. I wear clothes that will divert attention from my weight.	1	2	3	4	5	6
17. I avoid going clothes shopping.	1	2	3	4	5	6
18. I don't wear "revealing" clothes (e.g., bathing suits, tank tops, or shorts).	1	2	3	4	5	6
19. I get dressed up or made up.	6	5	4	3	2	1

Rosen, J.C., et al. (1991). Development of a Body Image Avoidance Questionnaire, Psychological Assessment, 3, 32–37. Used by permission.

Scoring Your Test

To find your score, simply add the numbers that you have circled and write your total on the line below.

Your Score _____

UNDERSTANDING YOUR SCORE

Your Score	Percentile	Body Image
19–42	15	Bathing suit! Are you kidding?
43–66	30	One-piece
67–84	50	Modest two-piece
85–96	70	Bikini
97–114	85	Thong

WHAT DOES YOUR SCORE MEAN?

Score of 19 to 66—"Bathing Suit! Are You Kidding?"

You are uncomfortable with your body and tend to hide in your clothes. You prefer the lights off and the clothes on. You are not a "disrober" in any context. You wouldn't be caught dead in a bathing suit—or anything less than modest dress. In fact, the more clothes on, the better you feel. Sometimes you avoid intimacy because you are concerned about your figure. Unfortunately, you permit your perception of your shape to dominate many of your decisions. Dieting and weight may be central to your friendships, but these may play too great a role in your conversations. Your body is a shell. Your personality is inside it. Rather than focusing on the harsh aspects of your body, concentrate on your attractive features. It is not helpful to berate yourself about your appearance. Accept your body as it is, as once you become comfortable with your body, so will others. If one of your goals is greater physical health, certainly work toward that, but in the meantime, agree to live in your body without loathing it. Take small steps toward improvement.

Score of 67 to 84—"Modest Two-piece"

Your view of your body is about average. While you are willing to show a glimpse of skin in public, the main show is for your partner's eyes only. You don't permit your body to always dictate your mood or actions, but you will forbid others from seeing your body on occasion. While at times you feel confident with your physique, most of the time you struggle for acceptance. You are aware of your flaws, but acceptance is the key here. You do not need a model's body to feel sexy. In fact, a little more comfort in your own skin will make you a much more sensual person. Come on, get in touch with your sexy side, none of us are perfect. Appreciating this will give you greater confidence.

Score of 85 to 114—"Bikini"

You are more daring and suggestive than two-thirds of the population. You are wonderfully comfortable with your body and this frees your mind to move in the direction of skimpy. Your bathing suit would earn you many glances as you walk along the beach. You feel good about your body in a healthy way. You may be comfortable enough with your body to be more naked than clothed. Perhaps you enjoy doing housework in the nude and do not mind if strangers catch a glimpse of you "au naturel." You do not necessarily have a model's body, but to you "bare is beautiful." While your confidence is commendable, please be aware that your bare-all attitude can make others uncomfortable.

Cravings

So frequently in our personality tour, we see how the mind can affect basic needs. Food cravings are another fine example. As you might imagine, there are times when the body calls out for nutrients for purely physical needs. Those are interesting enough, but when the mind gets involved . . . that is when human behavior turns quirky.

We will now pay a quick visit to food cravings and see how physical requirements differ from psychological needs . . .

GEOPHAGY

Food cravings can be the body's way of signaling a lack of certain nutrients. Hungry for bananas? Your body may be asking for potassium. Many of us are familiar with unusual cravings in pregnant women. These are thought to be the body's way of calling for nutrients. However, in various parts of Africa and the southeast United States, this need gets a little unusual. These pregnant and lactating women crave dirt. This widespread condition is known as *geophagy*. But not just any scoop of dirt will do—many families have favorite areas from which the clay is harvested. And as a special treat, some mothers in the southern United States and in areas of Africa will send their pregnant daughters packages of this natural nutritious supplement from the family site.

PICA

Other cravings are the result of psychological needs—unmet needs for fun and excitement, a desire for love and sexual satisfaction, a feeling of emptiness and loss of control, or the result

A TASTE FOR THE UNUSUAL—PICA

In 2004, the *New England Journal of Medicine* reported that a 62-year-old French man visited an emergency room with a severe belly ache. He was in extreme pain, could not eat, or move his bowels. Doctors X-rayed his stomach and found it missing—rather it had dropped down between his hips—due to the fact that it contained twelve pounds of coins, jewelry, and needles. Twelve pounds! The weight of a bowling ball. Apparently, the patient had been slipping coins into his mouth for the past ten years! Maybe he wanted a change in his diet, as his belly held 350 coins worth over $650. Don't try this at home: The Frenchman died within days of his surgery.

of excessive stress. Sometimes these cravings take on bizarre forms. One of the most unusual is known as Pica, a compulsion to eat things not normally consumed as food. Now it is okay for children to experiment with the unusual, they may like the feel of the objects in their mouths or imitate a dog for example. For the practice to be called Pica, the individual must maintain this habit for over one month. Common Pica snacks include cigarette butts, paint chips, coffee grounds, a side of glue, and soap for dessert!

Are Your Cravings Physical or Psychological?

Answer the following questions to help you decide if your craving is psychological or physiological:

Physical Needs	Psychological Needs
Do you eat certain foods because you experience a sudden lack of energy?	Do you crave something sweet after dinner?
Do you eat because there is a gnawing feeling in your stomach?	Do you have to have hot dogs at a ballgame or chips while watching TV?
Do you feel light-headed so you eat something?	Do you get hungry at the mention of ice cream?
Have you experienced the feeling where you can't stop thinking about meat, or spinach, or even fatty foods, etc.?	Do you often feel like you can't decide what you want to eat, but feel the need to eat something?
Do you crave foods that you would not normally eat or don't particularly enjoy?	Do you eat because you are stressed or bored?

If you mostly answered yes to these questions in the first column, your cravings are physical. If you mostly answered "yes" to the questions in the second column, they are psychological.

If you are trying to conquer attacks from psychological cravings, try these helpful hints. Pick one or two and see which works best for you.

1. Eat a light healthy snack every three hours.

2. Drink a glass of water every hour.

3. Make the cravings wait fifteen to twenty minutes before eating, they may dissipate.

4. Change your activity to distract your craving.

5. Exercise to help the craving disappear.

6. Change your routine. Turn the kitchen light off and avoid the room. Move your desk or sit differently. Sometimes a little physical exertion and a focused mind makes it easier to ride out the yearning.

EATING IDIOSYNCRASIES

We all have our little intake idiosyncrasies. Eating is far too ritualistic to permit us "normality." The following are common (and amusing) examples of eating quirks. Most readers will recognize someone they know in these curious consumption characters.

Texture Taboo Tony

Tony's eating habits are dictated by texture. He cannot eat food that is slimy or furry. For him, cooked spaghetti slithers down his throat, and okra becomes "alive" in his mouth. Don't even try to get him to eat a mushroom and keep that fuzzy peach on the tree.

Esthete Ester

Ester eats food according to her self-determined "ugliness scale." She eats the ugliest thing on her plate first and works her way toward the most attractive. If a piece of meat is not cut quite right, it's eaten first. An imperfect pea? Gone! A sloppy blob of mashed potatoes? Ingested in a flash! With each mouthful, the dish approaches a poster plate for Betty Crocker.

Clockwise Claudia

Claudia uses her dish as a clock and eats the food according to the hours. She sees her plate as a clock face with invisible hours around the circumference. She starts at high noon and eats everything between 12:00 and 1:00. She then moves on to the food between 1:00 and 2:00. Claudia continues clockwise until the plate is cleaned at midnight.

Hide-n-Seek Henry

Henry refuses to eat any concealed food. If he can't see it, it won't go anywhere near his mouth. Ravioli—forget it! There could be *anything* hiding in there! A jelly donut? Ugh! Henry does not tolerate culinary surprises.

Rainbow Rhonda

Watching Rhonda eat a bag of M&M's is a real treat, but you better have some time on your hands. Rhonda must sort all of the M&M's by color and then eat them in order. She will form her candies into a little graph then eat the color with the most remaining. Who would have thought that candy was brain food?

Billy the Blob

Billy loves french fries, but must have ketchup and mayonnaise with them. So he has a little cup on his left for ketchup, one on

The thought of something hidden in food
(like jelly in doughnuts) is frightening to some.

the right for mayo, and one in the middle for mixing the two. Precision is the key here, just the right amounts of each ingredient to make the perfect, pink paste.

Deb the Divider
Poor Deb, she would be horrified with Billy's behavior. Deb the divider is an isolationist. She breaks out in a cold sweat if her peas accidentally touch her mashed potatoes. And don't even ask about the gravy! Deb also washes her plate several times during a meal to ensure that she won't taste two foods together. Incidentally, like most food quirks, Deb learned hers at an early age. It seems that she is from a large farming family and every night Dad would plop a dollop of each food on the children's plates—including dessert! The entire meal was pushed on one plate and dispensed to the family. While Deb is a middle-aged professional now, she still recoils at the thought of her foods touching each other.

Helen the Hostess
While most hostesses are concerned with the mingling of the guests, Helen takes special care with the seating arrangements. She *must* find a pattern before anyone can eat. She may seat the guests according to shirt color or hair length. She may alternate long hair, short hair, etc., or she may cluster them in pairs, but she cannot eat until there is a clear pattern at her dinner table.

Mathematical Matt
Sixteen—thirty-two—Hut! Matt sets his life according to the numbers sixteen and thirty-two. His alarm goes off every morning at 6:32, *never* 6:30. He takes *exactly* thirty-two bites from his sandwich, chewing each bite *exactly* sixteen times before swallowing. Ever resourceful, he adjusts the size of his bites to ensure that every sandwich he eats, large or small, requires ex-

actly thirty-two bites to finish. Thankfully, his sex life does not have the same fixation.

The list of eating quirks is infinite, and while they run the risk of being annoying, that annoyance may be a little unfair. After all, table manners are really only peculiar rituals that have been adopted by enough people to make them "normal." Who decided that the salad fork is placed on the outside or that the water glass to your left is yours . . . or is it your right?

Of course, there are times when the behavior considered normal doesn't feel normal to you. What happens when the desire to lose a couple of pounds to impress your friends and potential partner grows into an obsession and takes control of your life? When does diet equal disorder?

Eating Disorders

No one wakes up one morning and suddenly has an eating disorder. It is a gradual descent into a boiling pot of isolation, fear, and panic. The harder you try to gain control, the further the disease pulls you under. In the United States, obesity is the most frequent eating predicament, however, it's considered a medical problem rather than a psychological one. Psychologically, the three most common eating disorders are:

Binge Eating Disorder
This disorder is characterized by out-of-control eating episodes, often completed alone, followed by feelings of guilt and disgust. According to the National Institutes of Health, this is the most common eating disorder. Almost six million Americans suffer with Binge Eating Disorder.

Maria is trying to diet. She wakes up each morning to the thought of what she will eat that day. Food is her main concern all day long. She tries to think of other things, but the forbidden food haunts her. Before the day is over, she rushes home, locks the door, and in the snap of a pretzel devours a bag of chips, a box of cookies, and a gallon of ice cream. This is a delightful time for Maria, but it's short-lived. Staring at the empty containers that litter her couch, she bursts into tears, demeaning herself. *How could I have eaten all that*?! Back to the diet again tomorrow for Maria.

Bulimia

Similar to binge eating, bulimia is uncontrolled eating followed by inappropriate compensatory behavior (vomiting, abusing laxatives, diuretics, enemas, fasting).

Nick is a wrestler. He almost made it to state last year. He knows he can win it all this year—if he just loses ten pounds. Although he only has 2 percent body fat, he can still achieve his goal by fasting. He chews on ice to help burn calories, but when his teammates cajole him into sharing some pizza or a couple of tacos, Nick gives in and enjoys time with his pals. However, soon after he finishes eating he sneaks away and forces himself to vomit. Water pills and laxatives also help him reach his goal. The problem is, there is always a lighter weight class and a new, lower, goal.

Anorexia Nervosa

This is self-imposed starvation. Tina is 5' 6" and weighs 98 pounds, but when she looks in the mirror all she sees is fat. She pinches her pallid skin and just knows there are globs of fat underneath. Her parents are concerned for their daughter and try to monitor her intake, but Tina is wily. She pushes food around on the plate, slips some into her pockets, and fills her napkin when no one is looking. Tina's total control of her body is killing her.

DO YOU HAVE AN EATING DISORDER?

There are three stages of eating disorders—early, middle, and late. The following questionnaire was adapted from the University of California, Santa Barbara.

Early Stages

Do you diet or fast weekly or monthly?   YES   NO

Are you frequently depressed because you feel fat?   YES   NO

Would you eat more than others if you didn't control yourself?   YES   NO

Do you feel "good" or "bad" according to how much you eat, how much you weigh, or how much exercise you get?   YES   NO

Do you purge occasionally to feel in control?   YES   NO

Middle Stages

Do you keep to yourself and feel lonely because you believe you are too fat?   YES   NO

Do you use laxatives, vomiting, diet pills, or water pills to help you lose weight or feel in control of your weight?   YES   NO

Are you frightened at the thought of eating situations where you will have to eat a normal meal?   YES   NO

Do you frequently eat beyond the point of fullness to the point of physical discomfort?   YES   NO

When you feel full, do you also feel self-hatred, desperation, panic or depression?   YES   NO

Late Stages

Are there certain foods that you trust not to stick to you, bloat you, or make you gain weight?   YES   NO

Do you secretly eat in such a way that your meals last longer or seem larger? For example, cutting each piece in tiny sections, or counting each mouthful as you eat?   YES   NO

Do you prefer to eat when you are home alone?   YES   NO

Do you use laxatives, vomiting, diet pills, or exercise whenever you eat "bad" foods?   YES   NO

When you eat in the presence of others, do you worry about how you're going to get rid of that meal?   YES   NO

Do you feel secretly proud when someone tells you that you're too thin?   YES   NO

In the early stage of an eating disorder, eating is becoming central to how you define happiness and achievement. By the middle stage, eating attitudes begin to affect your behavior. Notice in the middle stages of eating disorders, the clues that control overeating are lost. In the late stages, this loss of control escalates and secrecy plays a greater role in your eating decisions. It is in this secrecy where the greatest danger resides. While it is normal to answer "yes" to one or two of these items, if you find that you responded "yes" to more than three questions in any of the stages, you may be suffering from an eating disorder.

TEST YOURSELF

Instructions

These simple questions are designed to help you assess where you are in terms of healthy and unhealthy eating habits. There are only twenty-six statements on this test. Honestly consider each one. This test can help you better understand your feelings.

HOW DANGEROUS ARE YOUR EATING HABITS?

Circle the numbers below to indicate how frequently you engage in each behavior:

	Always	Usually	Often	Sometimes	Rarely	Never
1. I am terrified about being overweight.	3	2	1	0	0	0
2. I avoid eating when I am hungry.	3	2	1	0	0	0
3. I find myself preoccupied with food.	3	2	1	0	0	0
4. I have gone on eating binges where I feel that I may not be able to stop.	3	2	1	0	0	0
5. I cut my food into small pieces.	3	2	1	0	0	0
6. I am aware of the calorie content of foods that I eat.	3	2	1	0	0	0
7. I particularly avoid foods with a high carbohydrate content (i.e. bread, rice, potatoes, etc.)	3	2	1	0	0	0
8. I feel that others would prefer if I ate more.	3	2	1	0	0	0
9. I vomit after I have eaten.	3	2	1	0	0	0
10. I feel extremely guilty after eating.	3	2	1	0	0	0

	Always	Usually	Often	Sometimes	Rarely	Never
11. I am preoccupied with a desire to be thinner.	3	2	1	0	0	0
12. I think about burning up calories when I exercise.	3	2	1	0	0	0
13. Other people think that I am too thin.	3	2	1	0	0	0
14. I am preoccupied with the thought of having fat on my body.	3	2	1	0	0	0
15. I take longer than others to eat my meals.	3	2	1	0	0	0
16. I avoid foods with sugar in them.	3	2	1	0	0	0
17. I eat diet foods.	3	2	1	0	0	0
18. I feel that food controls my life.	3	2	1	0	0	0
19. I display self-control around food.	3	2	1	0	0	0
20. I feel that others pressure me to eat.	3	2	1	0	0	0
21. I give too much time and thought to food.	3	2	1	0	0	0
22. I feel uncomfortable after eating sweets.	3	2	1	0	0	0
23. I engage in dieting behavior.	3	2	1	0	0	0
24. I like my stomach to be empty.	3	2	1	0	0	0

	Always	Usually	Often	Sometimes	Rarely	Never
25. I enjoy trying new rich foods.	0	0	0	1	2	3
26. I have the impulse to vomit after meals.	3	2	1	0	0	0

Garner, D.M., Olmsted, M.P., Bohr, Y. and Garfinkel, P.E. (1982). The Eating Attitudes Test: Psychometric Features and Clinical Correlates. Psychological Medicine, 12, 871-878. Used by permission. (Information on the EAT can be found at www.river-centre.org.)

Scoring Your Test

To find your score, simply add the numbers that you have circled and write your total on the line below.

Your Score _____

UNDERSTANDING YOUR SCORE

The range of answers is from 0 to 78. The higher your score, the more you might be susceptible to an eating disorder. Due to the complex nature of eating attitudes and behavior, the averages of various groups are shown below. Use these numbers as indicators to understand your eating habits so you can modify them in a way that is more beneficial for you. If you think you might have a problem, speak with your physician.

HOW OTHERS SCORED

Group	Average Score
Men with no eating disorders	9
Women with no eating disorders	16
Obese men and women	17

Binge Eating Disorder	32
Bulimics	41
Anorexics	59

Alcoholism

No chapter on consumption conduct would be complete without a mention of alcohol. So, we shall finish off this delicious chapter with a drink. According to the United States Department of Health and Human Services, about half of the nation's adult population drinks alcohol and well over twenty million Americans abuse it. This next test is used frequently to detect alcohol abuse.

TEST YOURSELF

Instructions

This quick test consists of twenty-four simple questions. The most difficult part of this test may be the honesty required to take it. Like all forms of abuse, alcoholism is ugliest when it is left alone. If you are taking this test at the request of a loved one, please recognize it is because of their concern for you.

The test takes less than ten minutes to complete and each question only requires a "yes" or a "no" answer.

DOES YOUR DRINKING AFFECT YOUR LIFE?

Please circle either "yes" or "no" for each item as it applies to you:

	Yes	No
1. Do you feel you are a normal drinker?	0	2
2. Have you ever awakened the morning after drinking the night before and found that you could not remember a part of that evening?	2	0
3. Does your wife, husband, parent, or other near relative ever worry or complain about your drinking?	1	0
4. Can you stop drinking without a struggle after one or two drinks?	0	2
5. Do you ever feel guilty about your drinking?	1	0
6. Do friends or relatives think you are a normal drinker?	0	2
7. Are you able to stop drinking when you want to?	0	2
8. Have you ever attended a meeting of Alcoholics Anonymous (AA)?	5	0
9. Have you ever gotten into physical fights when drinking?	1	0
10. Has drinking ever created problems between you and your wife, husband, parent, or other near relative?	2	0
11. Has your wife, husband, parent, or other near relative ever gone to anyone for help about your drinking?	2	0
12. Have you ever lost friends or girlfriends/boyfriends because of your drinking?	2	0
13. Have you ever gotten into trouble at work because of drinking?	2	0

	Yes	No
14. Have you ever lost a job because of drinking?	2	0
15. Have you ever neglected your obligations, your family, or your work for two or more days in a row because you were drinking?	2	0
16. Do you drink before noon fairly often?	1	0
17. Have you ever been told you have liver trouble or cirrhosis?	2	0
18. After heavy drinking, have you ever had delirium tremens (DTs) or severe shaking, heard voices, or seen things that weren't really there?	5	0
19. Have you ever gone to anyone for help about your drinking?	5	0
20. Have you ever been in a hospital because of drinking?	5	0
21. Have you ever been a patient in a psychiatric hospital or on a psychiatric ward of a general hospital where drinking was part of the problem that resulted in hospitalization?	2	0
22. Have you ever been seen at a psychiatric or mental health clinic, or gone to a doctor, social worker, or clergyman for help with any emotional problem where drinking was part of the problem?	2	0
23. Have you ever been arrested for drunken driving while intoxicated or driving under the influence of alcoholic beverages?	2	0
24. Have you ever been arrested, even for a few hours, because of other drunken behavior?	2	0

Selzer, M.L. (1971). The Michigan Alcoholism Screening Test: The Quest for a New Diagnostic Instrument, American Journal of Psychiatry, 127(12):1653–8.

Scoring Your Test

Simply add the numbers that you have circled and write your total on the line below.

Your Score _____

UNDERSTANDING YOUR SCORE

Honest answers to these questions can effectively identify most people in need of alcohol counseling or treatment. It does not provide a diagnosis. If you have questions about your alcohol use, contact a physician or counselor.

Your Score	What Your Score Means . . .
0 to 3	You are a most valuable guest at any party—you are the designated driver! Your drinking habits score in the normal range, low risk.
4 to 9	Your score indicates that you are at risk for problem drinking. You may be addicted to alcohol. Contact a physician for help.
10 or More	If your answers are accurate, you have alcoholism. Contact a physician for help.

Consumption Summary

We are now at the end of the consumption segment of the personality tour. Do you know yet? Are you crazy? Have you been reminded of family, friends, or coworkers? To recap, we have gotten to know each other a little better. We learned whether you love yourself too much (narcissism), too little (negative labels), or just the right amount. We explored your relationships and measured your ability to love and relate to others. Then we went to dinner and discovered all the zany eating habits that go on behind closed doors. So, we've gotten to know each other, discussed our relationships, had dinner . . . I guess it is time for sex.

4.

sexual peccadilloes: fetishes, fantasies, and other naughty behaviors

Love is the answer—but while you're waiting for the answer, sex raises some pretty good questions.   **—WOODY ALLEN**

Nothing occupies our mind like sex. Our films, magazines, and television programs are brimming with sexual innuendos and encounters. Our music ranges from sappy love songs to explicit anthems. Adult book stores flourish and Passion Parties have now replaced the old Tupperware get-togethers. Sex is everywhere. According to the University of Cambridge Press, the English language now has over 2,500 words to describe genitals. That's ballsy. Sex is in the open, discussed at almost every gathering, from weddings to wakes. We are fascinated with sex. But wait a minute—isn't sex supposed to be private?

Procreation is our biological mission. The pleasures of intimacy bind the genders. Think about it, if sex was not fun, we wouldn't do it. Who would volunteer for all that sweat and smell and sinew? If sex did not feel so good, humans would have become extinct millennia ago. Instead we have added ten new humans to the planet in the time it took you to read this paragraph. There is something good about sex.

Our Sexual Identity

There seems to be no end to the inventiveness with which we engage in sexual relations. No limit to the permutations and positions, to the number and arrangement of partners, nor to the type of creative sexual expression. When it comes to sex, we are at our most creative.

With so much potential variety in sexual relations between consenting adults, who is to say what is right or normal? When we seek intimacy, we are looking for a connection, a kindred spirit, someone whose definition of normal is compatible with our own. Or maybe we're looking for someone to teach us a few things and expand our sexual horizons. And yet, no matter how wide our definition of normal, there are times when the complexity of our sexual nature confounds us. In extreme cases, our definition of normal is so far beyond society's boundaries that our chosen form of sexual expression breaks laws.

In this chapter, you will learn what makes you tick and discover just how wide is the range of sexual expression. Some parts of this section will excite you, some will enthrall, and others will repel you. When we get to the parts that make your stomach crawl, I merely ask that you permit yourself to walk a few steps in the shoes of those featured here in the hope that you come to better understand your neighbor.

HOW SEXUALLY AWARE ARE YOU?

Please read each item carefully and decide to what extent it is characteristic of you:

	Not at All	Slightly	Somewhat	Moderately	Very
1. I am very aware of my sexual feelings.	0	1	2	3	4
2. I'm very aware of my sexual motivations.	0	1	2	3	4
3. I'm very alert to changes in my sexual desires.	0	1	2	3	4
4. I am very aware of my sexual tendencies.	0	1	2	3	4
5. I'm very aware of the way my mind works when I'm sexually aroused.	0	1	2	3	4
6. I know what turns me on sexually.	0	1	2	3	4
7. I wonder whether others think I'm sexy.	0	1	2	3	4
8. I'm concerned about the sexual appearance of my body.	0	1	2	3	4
9. I usually worry about making a good sexual impression on others.	0	1	2	3	4
10. I'm concerned about what other people think of my sex appeal.	0	1	2	3	4
11. I rarely think about my sex appeal.	4	3	2	1	0

	Not at All	Slightly	Somewhat	Moderately	Very
12. I don't care what others think of my sexuality.	0	1	2	3	4
13. I rarely think about the sexual aspects of my life.	0	1	2	3	4
14. I don't think about my sexuality very much.	4	3	2	1	0
15. Other people's opinions of my sexuality don't matter very much to me.	4	3	2	1	0
16. I'm assertive about the sexual aspects of my life.	0	1	2	3	4
17. I'm not very direct about voicing my sexual desires.	4	3	2	1	0
18. I am somewhat passive about expressing my sexual desires	4	3	2	1	0
19. I do not hesitate to ask for what I want in a sexual relationship.	0	1	2	3	4
20. I'm the type of person who insists on having my sexual needs met.	0	1	2	3	4
21. When it comes to sex, I usually ask for what I want.	0	1	2	3	4
22. If I were to have sex with someone, I'd tell my partner what I like.	0	1	2	3	4

Snell, W.E., Jr. et al. (1991). Development of the Sexual Awareness Questionnaire: Components, Reliability, and Validity. Annals of Sex Research, 4, 65–92. Used by permission.

SCORING YOUR TEST

This is one of those delightfully sneaky tests that measure a little more than you expected. This test consists of three separate parts—each one will help you uncover a little of your sexual awareness.

To find your scores, simply add the numbers you circled and write your totals on the lines below.

Your Sexual Consciousness (questions 1 to 6) _____

Your Sexual Monitoring (questions 7 to 15) _____

Your Sexual Assertiveness (questions 16 to 22) _____

UNDERSTANDING YOUR SCORE

SEXUAL CONSCIOUSNESS

Your Score	Level of Sexual Consciousness
0-10	Unconscious
11-20	Semiconscious
21-24	Concentrating

WHAT DOES YOUR SCORE MEAN?
Score of 0 to 10—Wake Up and Smell the K-Y Jelly!!

Come on, there is a wild and wonderful series of sexual stimuli awaiting your brain. While you may enjoy sex, you are not introspective about your needs and desires. You are barely conscious when it comes to your sexual thoughts. Use your imagination. Think about what gets your engine revving. Reflect alone then talk with your partner about sex, explore your fantasies and motivations. Both you and your partner will be grateful.

Score of 11 to 20—In Touch

You are fairly in touch with sexual desires. Your score is about average in this department. You probably have a healthy sexual outlook and have had—or will have—rewarding relationships. You enjoy sex and enjoy thinking about sex, but sometimes you get a little lost because you have not fully explored your sexuality. There is a big, full world of experiences waiting for you, but you have to know what you want, then convey these wishes to your partner. Consider your intimate needs and explore them.

Score of 21 to 24—Hot Dog!!

You have wonderful introspective skills and know your needs. You have scored in the top group for sexual consciousness. You know your desires, abilities, and wishes. You are plugged in. If your partner has not scored quite as high as you, patiently facilitate their mental growth.

SEXUAL MONITORING

Your Score	Level of Sexual Monitoring
0-15	Oblivious
16-28	Observer
29-36	Overseer

WHAT DOES YOUR SCORE MEAN?

Score of 0 to 15—Don't Care

You really don't care what others think of your sexuality or may feel insecure in this area. Sensuality is something you barely consider yourself, but are aware of it in others. You may notice a skimpy outfit go by and be a tad bit envious or downright appalled. Displaying your sexual self is not something you are comfortable with. You probably dress to de-emphasize your sexuality.

If you are satisfied with people's reaction (or nonreaction) to your sexuality, fine. If you wish for a little more notice, you will have to start small and work on your comfort level. Even a killer outfit will look awkward if it is not worn with confidence. Pick your best feature and display it: your chest, in a low cut top or snug shirt; your butt, in a pair of tight jeans, or your legs, in shorts or a skirt.

Score of 16 to 28—Don't Know
You are aware of your sexual being, and will sometimes dress to impress. Although you probably own a few killer outfits that you wear on first dates or special occasions, you still prefer comfort over sexy. Allow yourself the freedom to explore your sexual identity even further. Realize that you can balance good taste with sexy—it will give you an aura of confidence.

Score of 29 to 36—Don't Try and Stop Me!!
Whoooweeee! Looking good is just one aspect of your arsenal. You dress to kill and take no survivors. You care about how you look, your sensuality is important to who you are, and you know how to work that thang!

If you scored very high here, there is a possibility that you may be too fixated on appearance and sex, and risk intimidating your partners. Additionally, be careful your self-esteem isn't over inflated. Arrogance is rarely a turn-on for anyone. Remember healthy sexual relationships are about give and take.

SEXUAL ASSERTIVENESS

Your Score	Level of Sexual Assertiveness
0-7	Hesitant
8-20	Secure
21-28	Assertive

WHAT DOES YOUR SCORE MEAN?

Score of 0 to 7—Stop

Passive, timid, unsure. Oh baby, there is a lifetime of great sex out there if you can communicate your needs to a loving partner. But you won't speak up. Perhaps you don't know what you want or you believe that sex is bad or sinful. Regardless, you have the brakes on your sensual life. If you want to make a change, start with some self-exploration. Contemplate your desires, then speak with your partner about them. You may be surprised at how well things turn out.

Score of 8 to 20—Proceed with Caution

As far as sexual assertiveness goes, your score is about average. This means that you have a fairly healthy, basic notion of your needs, but may be reluctant in communicating them to your partner. If you wish to be more in touch with your sensual side, read and learn about the possibilities. Consider which desires are not addressed in your relationship, then pick a time when you and your partner are quietly cuddling and communicate those needs. If you are shy about making your needs known, discreetly leave out a magazine where your wishes are discussed. Try non-verbal communication. Leave a little teasing note or place your partner in the position you want and gesture subtly.

Score of 21 to 28—You Go!

You know what you want and you go for it! You are direct, decisive, and dominant. Sex with you is great, as you know your needs and see that they are met. Not only that, but you are marvelously sexually independent. You rely on your own opinions when making intimacy choices. You have got it together. Be careful that you are not so dominant and self-absorbed that you are not in tune to your partner's desires. If you balance your wants with your lover's, then you are a true sexual partner.

Triggers: Let the Good Times Roll!

Understanding yourself is the first step in finding sexual satisfaction in a relationship. Unfortunately, almost one-third of all married couples are dissatisfied with their sex life. The main culprit is fatigue. We are busy with our careers, shuffling the children to their activities, maintaining the house and yard, and eventually something has to give. We find little time for ourselves, let alone the chance to cozy up with our partner.

So, if your partner is too tired or perhaps a little bored, how can you jump-start their libido? Here are some sexy ideas to trigger your partner's drive.

MASSAGE

If your partner is tired, nothing feels better than a good full-body massage. Be sure to engage all of the senses in your body exploration—a little soft music to caress the ears; the sight of flickering candlelight glowing on your partner's skin; the delicate scent of body oils tease the nose. Start at the top and slowly work your way down, hitting the pressure points—neck, shoulders, each vertebrae of the spine, and the hands. Don't forget those tired feet and toes before you advance to the erogenous zones.

SENSUAL SENSES

In addition to biological regions, there is a psychology to love-making. Consider how your partner's mind enjoys the following:

THE BACK AND NECK MASSAGE WERE FOR YOU. THIS IS FOR ME!

DO YOU KNOW YOUR EROGENOUS ZONES?

While this is not cause for diagnosis and medication, if you don't know your erogenous zones by now you should! Study these and get some hands-on experience.

There are two types of erogenous zones: Scientifically, these are called the "specific" and "nonspecific," but it is easier to think of them as the hairy and the nonhairy areas. Nonspecific zones are general areas of skin, with hair, that enjoy a good tickling. Specific zones are those hairless, special areas packed with nerve endings that tingle when touched.

Making love is like enjoying a smorgasbord; enjoy a little taste of the variety. This list works for both men and women . . .

- Lips
- Breasts
- Nipples
- Buttocks
- Anus
- Genitals
- G-spot/prostate

- Scalp
- Nape of neck
- Navel
- Inner thigh
- Back of knees
- Feet
- Toes

- Ears
- Ribs
- Hips
- Armpits
- Wrists
- Hands
- Fingers

When lovemaking is done right, the entire body becomes erogenous. The surface of the skin, the blood pulsating in your lover's body, down to the thoughts racing and floating through your partner's mind.

Water

There is something erotic about water, whether it is a hot tub, the ocean, or a warm shower. Maybe it is because you are squeaky clean. Maybe it is the feel of the dampness against your skin, the warm cocoon encompassing your body. Also, consider the soft sounds of waves tumbling onto a beach or water trickling down smooth stones. Whatever it is, water can be a turn-on. So, grab your partner and a glass of wine and head for a bubble bath.

Alcohol

Alcohol in moderation relaxes our muscles, reduces our inhibitions, and releases our minds. A friend confided that he loved it when he saw his wife have a beer or glass of wine as he knew she would be amorous that night. Enjoying a sip of champagne off your partner's body is also an erotic experience.

Food

We saw in the previous chapter how our minds and food connect. Here are a few more fun examples.

- Chocolate—The Aztec ruler, Montezuma, drank fifty cups of chocolate each day to better serve his harem. Seventeenth-century church officials deemed it sinful to consume chocolate. Scientifically, we know chocolate contains phenylethylamine, the same molecule that courses through our veins when we are in love.

- Asparagus—If a food looks sexual, it will aid sex. Asparagus is a beautiful phallic symbol. In the past, French lovers dined on three courses of it the night before their wedding. Packed with vitamins, it offers the love-hungry extra energy.

- Chiles—Eating peppers gets the blood rushing, the heart pumping, the face flushing, and the pores sweating. Sound familiar?

- Grapes—Ever since Marc Anthony first fed Cleopatra grapes, these plump bites of juice have been used to entice one another. They squirt a fountain of aphrodisiacal power right into your mouth, so savor them well.

- Honey—The Bible and Kama Sutra relate honey to love and sex. Tradition in India has a bridegroom consuming honey on his wedding day. In fact, Attila the Hun drank himself to death with honey on his honeymoon. Even the word honey conjures up the sensual image of a dripping, sticky substance on your lover's body, ready to be licked off. Sweet idea!

- Avocado—When cut in half, the pear shape resembles the curves of a woman, and then it melts on the tongue with a taste of its own. In Aztec culture, village maidens were forbidden to go outside as the fruit was being gathered because it was deemed so powerful.

- Any food can arouse your partner if care is taken in the way it is eaten—licking an ice cream cone, peeling a banana, or being creative with a french fry.

A CHANGE WILL DO YOU GOOD

It could be that all you need is a change of pace—or even place. Instead of the bed, try the living room, kitchen table, outside in the hammock, the backseat of your car. After dark, grab a blanket and head to your favorite golf course. The fear of getting caught can be an added thrill. A change of scenery will spark that desire and make everything feel new again.

GAMES

A sexual challenge can trigger the competitive spirit and rev up the imagination. The obvious solution is a game of strip poker. But what about a game of darts or pool where the winner is granted sexual favors? Board games abound that allow couples to explore their sexual fantasies. Don't have a board game? Create your own fun. Make a wish list where each partner writes down five desires. Put them in a hat and draw one, then act on it! Be sure to save the others for the next time.

WAIT! I STILL HAVE THIRTY SECONDS TO CHANGE MY MIND.

THREE MINUTE RULE

Here is a handy little idea to trigger a tired partner—agree to the Three Minute Rule. Since a lack of energy may be preventing your partner from embracing your sexy ideas, ask your mate to give you three minutes to change their mind. Use your three minutes to entice your partner. Engage all the senses, kiss and communicate your wishes, whisper sweet nothings, work those sweet spots. If after three minutes, they are still not in the mood, gracefully call it quits. However, you may find that after a few moments of special pampering, your partner will beg for more.

DISCOVER YOUR OWN BODY

Gone are the days of warning adolescents that they will go blind if they touch themselves. According to a University of Chicago study, the average eighteen- to forty-year-old male pleases himself at least twice a week; for women, it is roughly once a week. This is a normal activity; in fact it is encouraged as a method for getting comfortable with your own body. Some couples find masturbating in front of each other incredibly sexy and can be a terrific trigger. As Woody Allen put it "Don't knock masturbation, it is sex with someone I love."

Your Sexual Attitudes

Okay, we have learned how important sex is to our species, how in-touch and conscious you are of your sexual needs, and even a few fun "how to" ideas. Before we move onto mind-jarring sex peccadilloes, let's find out whether you are ready for the quirks . . .

TEST YOURSELF

Instructions

This test measures your attitudes about sex and society. It will tell you how conservative or liberal you are in your sexual beliefs. This test is particularly handy to explore issues with your partner. If you are in a romantic relationship, ask your partner to complete this test then discuss your differences and celebrate your similarities.

Merely circle the number that best represents how much you agree with each statement. The test should take you about ten minutes, but feel free to take longer. Just be honest and try to answer with the first opinion that comes to mind. There is no need to overthink these.

WHAT IS YOUR POSITION ON SEX?

For each of the following, please circle the number that best reflects your reaction to that statement.

	Strongly Disagree	Somewhat Disagree	Neutral	Somewhat Agree	Strongly Agree
1. Nudist camps should be made completely illegal.	5	4	3	2	1
2. Abortion should be made available whenever a woman feels it would be the best decision.	1	2	3	4	5
3. Information and advice about contraception (birth control) should be given to any individual who intends to have intercourse.	1	2	3	4	5
4. Parents should be informed if their children under the age of eighteen have visited a clinic to obtain a contraceptive device.	5	4	3	2	1
5. Our government should try harder to prevent the distribution of pornography.	5	4	3	2	1
6. Prostitution should be legalized.	1	2	3	4	5
7. Petting (a stimulating caress of any or all parts of the body) is immoral behavior unless the couple is married.	5	4	3	2	1
8. Premarital sexual intercourse for young people is unacceptable to me.	5	4	3	2	1

	Strongly Disagree	Somewhat Disagree	Neutral	Somewhat Agree	Strongly Agree
9. Sexual intercourse for unmarried young people is acceptable, without affection existing, if both partners agree.	1	2	3	4	5
10. Homosexual behavior is an acceptable variation in sexual preference.	1	2	3	4	5
11. A person who catches a sexually transmitted disease is probably getting exactly what he/she deserves.	5	4	3	2	1
12. A person's sexual behavior is his/her own business, and nobody should make value judgments about it.	1	2	3	4	5
13. Sexual intercourse should only occur between two people who are married to each other.	5	4	3	2	1

Fisher, T. D., and Hall, R. G. (1988). A Scale for the Comparison of Sexual Attitudes of Adolescents and Their Parents. The Journal of Sex Research, 24, 90–100. Used by permission.

Scoring Your Test

To find your score simply add up the numbers you circled and write the sum below.

Your Score: _____

Your Score	Your Sexual Attitude
Less than 27	Puritanical
27-34	Prude
35-52	Perfect
53-60	Passionate
More than 60	Permissive

WHAT DOES YOUR SCORE MEAN?

Score of 13 to 34—Properly Prudish

Some people may consider you a prude or terribly old-fashioned. You tend to have conservative opinions on sexual behavior and prefer long-term, monogamous relationships. You believe our intimate lives should be kept personal, and you're occasionally astounded by the comments and confessions of others. Be sure to show some tolerance and be willing to accept that others have different ideas and values about sex, even if you don't share those views.

Score of 35 to 52—Tactfully Tolerant

As far as sexual politics go, you prefer the middle of the road. Your sexual opinions are about average for many Americans. Although you have definite opinions, you are the type of person who is open to discussion and who can see both sides of sex issues. While you may not agree with the choices others make, you are tolerant and a good friend.

Score of 53 to 65—Laissez-faire Liberal

Open-minded, accepting, and experimental are all words that describe your views on sex. You are an uninhibited lover who is not constrained by social mores and peer pressure. You have a healthy live-and-let-live approach to sex. And your credo, "If it feels good do it," means you are hot between the sheets. While you believe that life would be better if people had more sex, you sometimes have a problem developing the more meaningful aspects of a relationship.

Coital Curiosities

Now we know more about your desires and expectations, let's move along to some . . . um,...ah . . . well, we'll call them distinctive sexual needs. The lower your score on the previous test, the harder it will be to explore desires that are different than yours, but understanding the human condition is important. Let's peek into the lives of those with "nonnormative forms of sexuality" or abnormal sex needs.

FETISHES: THE OBJECTS OF MY DESIRE
A fetish is a fixation on an object or body part to achieve sexual gratification. The fetishist becomes aroused by seeing, feeling, or smelling the desired object. Common fetishes include shoes, intimate apparel, silk, fur, gloves, rubber, leather, or feathers. A picture of the object may be used, however, the presence of the actual object is preferred. A fetishist may integrate the object into a sexual activity with a willing partner, such as using a feather to tickle the partner's body. Men are more easily conditioned to pair sex with objects, while women are more aroused by textures, sounds, and scents. There is no harm in incorporating a fetish into a little afternoon delight. Sometimes, however, a fetish develops to the point of a requirement for sexual satisfaction, this is when the hobby is labeled as a problem.

PARTIAL TO PARTIALISM?
Do you have the urge to reach out and squeeze your partner's tush every time they walk by? Do you prefer redheads? Are you a breast man or a leg woman? Does the idea of massaging the

DO YOU HAVE A FETISH?

As Dave Barry says: "There is a very fine line between 'hobby' and 'mental illness.'" Read the questions below, the more "yes" answers you have, the more active your hobby. If you answer "yes" to some of the first five questions and at least one of the last three questions, your interest is a full-blown fetish.

Are there certain inanimate objects such as leather goods, rubber, lingerie, or shoes that heighten your sexuality?   YES NO

Does the sexual attractiveness of an object increase if it has been worn or handled by another?   YES NO

Do you think often of sexual acts that include specific objects?   YES NO

Do you incorporate specific objects into most or all of your sexual encounters?   YES NO

Do you masturbate to the sight, feel, or smell of an object?   YES NO

Have you derived pleasure from a certain object for six months or longer?   YES NO

Does including a specific object interfere with your sexual life in an important way?   YES NO

Does your interest in specific objects cause significant problems in your relationships with others?   YES NO

penis between the soles of the feet or between the breasts stimulate you? Partialism is a form of a fetish which comes from body parts—hair, feet, legs, breasts, buttocks—you name it. If you separate the parts from the person, you are on the road to partialism. Partialism is more than the preference for blondes to brunettes. This fascination develops in adolescence and must last for six months or longer. More importantly, it must cause distress, lead to the loss of friends, and interfere with your job.

THE LIFE OF A FOOTIE

Norman is a nice enough guy. He works hard, has a good sense of humor, he's a great dad, his lovely wife, Cindy, adores him, but once the bedroom door closes . . . well, let's go to the window and take a closer look. For Norman to be in the mood, all it takes is for Cindy to run her foot up his pant leg. At night, when many couples are sitting in bed watching TV, Norm is lying on the floor as Cindy sits on the edge of the bed resting her feet on his face. Cindy is a pretty woman who cares for her appearance, but this does not matter to Norm—provided those feet are impeccable. This means no calluses or bunions, and toenails must be clipped to a specific length. Besides being an expert on foot massages, Norm gives the perfect pedicure. He likes this task. To him it is foreplay. His sexual encounters focus solely on caressing, smelling, and nibbling on those tasty tootsies. While Norm tries to please Cindy, he can only achieve orgasm by having his penis rubbed by her feet. A technique they call a "foot job."

In many ways, Norman is lucky to have found Cindy. While she loves him dearly, in some ways she feels like a foot widow. Occasionally, she wonders what would happen if she were in a car accident and lost her feet. She wishes Norm could understand that she is more than the sum of her parts, but Cindy learned about the foot fetish after they had been dating for a while and, gosh, everything else about him is just right for her.

After eight years of marriage, Cindy has learned a few tricks of her own. If Norm wants her to get a new pair of shoes, Cindy makes sure she gets the outfit to match them. When they have an occasional tiff, she just crosses her legs and begins massaging her own feet (this is like watching masturbation to Norm). Cindy has learned to enjoy the pampering as she knows Norm won't kick this habit.

Fantasies

With sex frequently in our thoughts, what things come to mind? One of our most common fantasies is oral sex. Whereas it used to be considered taboo, today it is considered conventional. Whereas our parents went to Tupperware© parties, today we have sex-toy parties. Tomorrow? Who knows, perhaps "rainbow parties." Currently, a small portion of United States teens participate in rainbow parties, where each female participant sports a different shade of lipstick and then performs oral sex on each male guest, thus creating a rainbow effect.

It might blow you away to know that while almost 70 percent of eighteen- to forty-four-year-old females enjoy a genital kiss, men provide stiff competition as 90 percent desire this attention.

Another popular fantasy is group sex. Some couples may joke, discuss, even role-play this scenario, but realize it will never be a reality. Others act. Open discussion prior to the experience will aid the success of it. Decide the parameters to ensure no jealousy. Do you prefer stranger or friend? What actions are allowed? Have a signal to ensure that both parties remain comfortable with the situation.

Do you have a secret fantasy of cowboys and construction workers? How about having sex with a cheerleader? Role-playing can add a new dimension to your sex life. So dust off that French maid outfit and give it a try.

Sharing and acting out fantasies increases intimacy as fan-

ORAL SEX BY THE BOOK

The more education you have, the more oral sex you enjoy.

Percent of American Adults Who Have Ever Received Oral Sex

	Women	Men
Not finished high school	50%	61%
High school graduate	67%	77%
Some college	82%	84%

Source: Sex in America: A Definitive Survey by Robert Michael et al. Little Brown & Co 1994

tasies become a shared secret between just the two of you. These can improve the performance and quality of your relationship. While fantasies are fun, please remember that being in the moment with your partner strengthens the bond of your relationship.

PARAPHILIA: FROM KIND TO KINKY

Paraphilia is a disorder characterized by recurrent and intense sexual fantasies and behaviors. Paraphilias are considered deviant because they involve objects or activities not considered sexually arousing to most people. With a paraphilia, the individual's urges and behaviors can lead to significant distress and sometimes criminal behavior. In some cases, individuals have urges or fantasies, but do not act on them. People with a paraphilia are usually unable to sustain a healthy, loving relationship.

Paraphilias are fairly rare and, for some reason, almost always affect men. This may be because men are visually stimulated, indiscriminately aroused, and orgasm-driven. The list of paraphilias includes, but is not limited to: sexual sadism/masochism, pedophilia, fetishism, transvestism, voyeurism, frotteurism, and exhibitionism.

Exhibitionism: Show and Tell

Phil, a twenty-four-year-old carpenter, spends much of his free time at the movie theater. Though not really interested in the latest theatrical release, Phil considers the theater a good place to expose himself to unsuspecting victims. Dressed in nothing but an overcoat, Phil buys a ticket to the latest "chick flick," and then finds a seat close to a woman—and near an exit. During the movie, Phil unties his coat and exposes his genitals to the woman. Phil derives sexual pleasure from his one-man show.

The primary intent of an exhibitionist is to evoke shock or fear in their victims, not necessarily to achieve an erection.

Though sexual contact is rare, an exhibitionist may masturbate while exposing himself. The risk of capture by the police may add an element of arousal for the exhibitionist. Most men who become exhibitionists succumb to this urge before they are eighteen years old. The condition becomes less severe after the age of forty.

Voyeurism: Keeping an Eye on You

Ian is a thirty-three-year-old bachelor who lives on the tenth floor of an apartment building. His living room has a wonderful view . . . of another tenant's bedroom.

Fortunately for Ian, the woman who lives in that opposing apartment isn't aware of the need to close her window blinds while undressing. Ian has established his routine around the woman's dressing schedule. At approximately 11:00 p.m. three times a week, Ian turns out his lights and masturbates while watching his neighbor undress. Recently, he even purchased a telescope to enhance his viewing pleasure. Ian experiences extra thrills while watching the sexual activities of his neighbor and her dates.

On occasion, Ian crosses paths with his neighbor in the parking lot, but he never acknowledges her. Voyeurs—or "Peeping Toms" as they are commonly known—do not seek to have sexual relations with the person they observe. They prefer to remain anonymous.

Oh, oh!! Ian has seen us looking in his bedroom window! We are voyeurs to a voyeur. Quick, head down to the subway . . .

Frotteurism: Don't Rub Me the Wrong Way

David works behind the scenes in a bank. He lives in the city and commutes to and from work via the subway. While most people dislike the crowded subway, David revels in the crush of humanity. The jostling mass of bodies allows David to bump into women, rubbing his genitals against their bodies. He wears plastic wrap around his concealed penis to keep his trousers clean. David suffers from frotteurism, a condition in which a person's sexual urges are related to touching or rubbing his genitals against the body of a nonconsenting individual. These close encounters often take place in crowded public settings. One of David's favorite haunts is by the subway turnstiles where he can arouse himself as he spots his next victim, once she enters the turnstile he quickly presses in behind her. David dashes off as soon as the gate opens. But here's the rub—David, like most frotteurists, fantasizes about loving, caring relationships with the women he accosts. In a sense, his goal is one that society encourages, but his methods are illegal. Incidentally, most frotteurists are younger, shy, inhibited men between fifteen and twenty-five years old.

Bestiality: You're an Animal!

Little girls love riding ponies and sleeping with teddy bears. We read our children tales in which the beautiful maiden kisses a frog, hoping she's found her prince. We all know how Beauty falls for the Beast. Seamen see mermaids, women love the feel of fur coats against their skin, young boys get ants in their pants. And where did all our stories of centaurs (half human, half horse) and satyrs (half human, half goat) and sphinx (human head, lion body) come from? Why do women report that men act like dogs and have cocks while men respond that chicks have pussies and beavers? And how come we all have asses? Let's face it our culture is brimming with bestiality. However, it is never discussed.

While the stereotypical bestiality encounter involves titters about farm boys and sheep, let's get realistic for a moment and spend a little time with Misty. Misty is a thirty-something, office-something, for a large corporate-something. She's the shy kind of awkward girl you pass right by in the hall and not even notice. Misty has had little success with men, she just doesn't have that spark to catch a fellow's interest. In fact, she gave up trying about five years ago. However, Misty does have Max. Max is a healthy, vibrant, fun-loving Labrador. When Misty first got a dog, one of her friends joked that now that she has Max to clean up after, she doesn't need a man.

Turns out Misty doesn't need a man. Misty was so pleased to have a companion, she liked it when Max laid his head on her lap while she read each night. Although he'd hog the bed most nights, Misty soon got used to the heavy body on the bed and the sound of his deep breaths as he snoozed next to her. Max gave Misty a warm, protected, loving feeling that she never had before.

Every once in a while on a quiet evening Misty would go to bed early and masturbate. A couple of times Max sniffed around as dogs do, and she had to push the big galoot off of her. Then one night Max licked Misty's vulva just as she was about to climax. The feeling was so intense, Misty had never experienced anything so powerful before. The next day she put the experience out of her mind. "Ugh, how dreadful!" she thought. She felt guilty and shameful. But somehow, over the next few months, Max learned to provide Misty with cunnilingus and analingus. Now, Misty is more satisfied than ever and none of her friends know just how much she loves that dog.

Bondage: When to Show Restraint

If you enjoy being all tied up with no place to go, bondage may be your secret pleasure. Bondage is a form of sexual practice that involves being tied up, restrained, or controlled by another for pleasure. The "for pleasure" part is important, as bondage is not about pain or torture, but trust. There are several rules to follow for a truly stimulating bondage experience.

DOS AND DON'TS FOR GOOD BONDAGE

Do	Don't
Each participant must completely trust the other.	Don't do anything that could cause physical or mental injury.
Physically and emotionally please the subject.	Don't obstruct breathing or circulation.
Use a gentle blindfold to enhance the subject's experience.	Do not permit the subject to escape.
Use a little humor.	Do not permit others to view subject.
Surprise the subject with treats like a feather, ice cube, or whipped cream	Don't say or do anything mean-spirited or cruel.

Remember: The goal is to share the joys of trust and physical pleasure. Make the experience a delightful one, and it may be reciprocated.

Sex studies show that about half of men and many women find bondage to be an erotic form of play. Psychologically, the eroticism of being bound derives from relinquishing all control. The subject can enjoy a totally guilt-free sexual experience. After all, if we are not in control, we can't be held responsible. If you are in a trusting relationship, give it a try. Bondage is only a paraphilia if it interferes with your life. So, pass the soft rope and enjoy the sweet surrender.

Sadism & Masochism: A Little Give and Take
All day long, Christine takes orders as she waits tables at a local diner. At night, however, she turns the tables and gives orders,

orchestrating activities most of us only read about in tawdry novels or witness vicariously in low-budget, racy movies. Christine is a sadist, sexually excited by inflicting pain—psychological or physical—on others. Her lair is located in the basement of her home, where she stores her special equipment. Her sex "toys" include whips, ropes, knives, nipple clamps, and razors. Christine enjoys tying up her playthings, spanking and whipping them while she yells epithets at them: "You've been a bad boy! Haven't you?"

Sadism differs from rough sex. Sadism is obtaining pleasure from inflicting physical or emotional pain on others. Christine obtains sexual arousal from her victim's pain. She enjoys the sense of being in complete control of her victim. Sadists get little pleasure from simulated pain, their thirst is for the real thing.

If you like to give your partner a little pat on the tush from

---

ARE YOU A SADIST?

There is a world of difference between giving your partner a spank on the tush during sex and being a sadist. If you answer "yes" to these questions, you are a sadist.

Over the past six months, have you had recurring, intense, sexual fantasies or urges in which you cause psychological or physical suffering to another?　YES　NO

Over the past six months, have you acted on sexual urges with a nonconsenting person?　YES　NO

Over the past six months, have your sexual urges to inflict psychological or physical suffering on another caused significant problems in your relationships or your ability to relate to others?　YES　NO

---

time to time, you are not a sadist. You will not slide down the slippery slope to sadism by spanking your consenting spouse every once in a while. Sadistic sexual fantasies generally begin in childhood with the onset of activities beginning as a young adult.

Bernie is a quiet man, often described by his coworkers at the CPA firm as a loner. Unbeknownst to his coworkers, Bernie leads a completely different life at night. A masochist, Bernie derives sexual gratification from being humiliated and abused and pays frequent visits to a sexual sadist, like Christine. Bernie loves being chained, gagged, and at the mercy of his partner. He finds himself sexually stimulated by verbal threats and insults, and enjoys his "bad boy" spankings. When Bernie is unable to visit his partner, he sometimes acts out his fantasies on himself—cutting and burning his skin.

Dominants and Submissives: From Top to Bottom A sadist/masochist relationship might be confused with a dominant/submissive pairing. We've all seen representations of the leather-clad "mistress" and her willing slave. More often, the dominant (top) and the submissive (bottom) merely enjoy the role-playing aspects of their sexual power games. In these situations, neither top nor bottom is interested in doling out or receiving actual physical pain or injury. Often, the role-playing provides a relief from real-world stresses.

Peter is a classic Type A business executive, always in control of his corporate surroundings, burdened with major responsibilities, including the welfare of his company and its many employees. He's always in charge and must lead with confidence and charisma.

Once Peter abandons the boardroom for the bedroom, however, he becomes the willing "bottom" in a dominant/submissive relationship that lets him completely surrender control by complying with his mistress's every wish and whim. None of these nocturnal decisions are his to make. During these few hours, in the midst of his secret fantasy, he can truly relax and enjoy himself.

Autoerotic Asphyxiation   Autoerotic asphyxiation is a dangerous masochistic activity in which someone may use ropes or plastic bags to interrupt breathing at the point of orgasm. A person who practices this is attempting to enhance orgasm, but sometimes this practice results in accidental death.

Sexual Addiction

Now, as we leave the quaint village of sexual quirks, we stop at the pharmacy on the outside of town and speak for a moment about addiction. If your sexual activities fill you with guilt and shame, or regret and self-loathing, you are missing one of the key components of healthy and loving relationships. Sex should be an enjoyable and pleasurable experience between consenting adults. Sexual addiction is any sexually related, compulsive behavior which hinders your life in meaningful ways. Sexual urges are considered addictions when they cause severe stress on your relationships with friends, family, and loved ones; impede the quality of your life to the extent that they interfere with your work; or place your life and the lives of others in danger by your actions. We'll begin an honest self-assessment by taking the sexual addiction test . . .

TEST YOURSELF

Instructions

This test measures your sexual history and behaviors. There are twenty-five yes/no questions. Merely read each question and honestly circle the number that best represents your experience. The test should take you about five minutes.

ARE YOU ADDICTED TO SEX?

Please answer yes or no to each question.

1. Were you sexually abused as a child or adolescent?   YES   NO

2. Do you regularly purchase romance novels or sexually explicit magazines?   YES   NO

3. Have you stayed in romantic relationships after they have become emotionally or physically abusive?   YES   NO

4. Do you often find yourself preoccupied with sexual thoughts or romantic daydreams?   YES   NO

5. Do you feel that your sexual behavior is not normal?   YES   NO

6. Does your spouse/significant other(s) worry or complain about your sexual behavior?   YES   NO

7. Do you have trouble stopping your sexual behavior when you know it is inappropriate?   YES   NO

8. Do you ever feel bad about your sexual behavior?   YES   NO

9. Has your sexual behavior ever created problems for you and your family?   YES   NO

10. Have you ever sought help for sexual behavior you did not like?   YES   NO

11. Have you ever worried about people finding out about your sexual activities?   YES   NO

12. Has anyone been hurt emotionally because of your sexual behavior?   YES   NO

13. Have you ever participated in sexual activity in exchange for money or gifts?   YES   NO

14. Do you have times when you act out sexually followed by periods of celibacy (no sex at all)?   YES   NO

15. Have you made efforts to quit a type of sexual activity and failed?   YES   NO

16. Do you hide some of your sexual behavior from others?   YES   NO

17. Do you find yourself having multiple romantic relationships at the same time?   YES   NO

18. Have you ever felt degraded by your sexual behavior?   YES   NO

19. Has sex or romantic fantasies been a way for you to escape your problems?   YES   NO

20. When you have sex, do you feel depressed afterwards?   YES   NO

21. Do you regularly engage in sadomasochistic behavior?   YES   NO

22. Has your sexual activity interfered with your family life?   YES   NO

23. Have you been sexual with minors?   YES   NO

24. Do you feel controlled by your sexual desire or fantasies of romance?   YES   NO

25. Do you ever think your sexual desire is stronger than you are?   YES   NO

Carnes, Patrick (1997–2003). *The Sexual Addiction Screening Test, Woman's Sexual Addiction Screening Test, and the Gay and Bisexual Male Sexual Addiction Screening Test. Used by permission.*

Scoring Your Test

Simply add the number of "yes" answers you circled and write your total on the line below. You get one point for every "yes."

Your Score _____

UNDERSTANDING YOUR SCORE

The results of this test do not prove (or disprove) that you are addicted to sex. This test provides an indicator of addiction, much like a barometer shows that bad weather may be coming. Use your test results as a screening device. The higher your score, the more likely it is that you have or will develop a problem.

WHAT DOES YOUR SCORE MEAN?

Score of 0 to 9—Sweet Melody

If you scored between 0 and 9, it is unlikely you are a sex addict. You probably have a healthy sexual outlook. You treat sex and your sexual partners responsibly. You have a low predisposition toward sexual addiction. Enjoy!

Score of 10 to 12—Soulful Tunes

Scores in the 10 to 12 range suggest that either you have done some things that you now regret or that you may be in an early stage of addiction. Maybe you take risks and you may enjoy living dangerously, but beware of the real potential for trouble ahead. At times, you may feel your sex life is out of control or unsatisfying. Sex can't cure depression or low self-esteem. You may need to free yourself from bad relationships. A competent counselor can help you learn to fight self-destructive impulses.

Score of 13 and Above—You're Gonna Have to Face It, You're Addicted to Love

Over 95 percent of sex addicts get a score of over 13 on this test. If you scored 13 or more, your experiences may be similar to those who are sex addicts. Chances are you have engaged in unhealthy, high-risk sexual activities. You may be jeopardizing important aspects of your life. Please seek counseling with a professional who understands sexual addiction.

Sexual Anorexia

We saw in the eating chapter how people can overconsume to become food or alcohol addicts; conversely, some become anorexic and starve themselves. Sexual anorexia is like this. It is an obsession where avoiding sex dominates your life. Those suffering

---

ARE YOU A SEXUAL ANOREXIC?

Sexual anorexics, like food anorexics, will starve themselves due to a distorted view of reality. They are plagued with feelings like these:

- Persistent fear of sexual encounters
- Abhorrence of sexual pleasure
- Fanatical concern for the sex lives of others
- Avoiding all things sexual
- Intense repugnance of their body functions
- Distorted view of their body
- Rigid opinions about sexual behavior

---

with sexual anorexia see the avoidance of sex as the solution to their problems. Sex becomes an enemy and constant vigilance is necessary. There are many similarities between sexual and food anorexics: They both starve themselves when sustenance is plentiful, both have distorted views of reality, and similarly, some sex anorexics will binge, then purge—they go through phases of extreme sexual promiscuity then follow up with total celibacy.

Asexuals

Sexual anorexics should not be confused with asexuals. We tend to consider individuals as either straight or gay, but there is an often overlooked third orientation—asexuality, those people who have absolutely no interest in sex. According to Canadian and British studies, approximately 1 percent of the population never feels sexual attraction. It is important to realize that asexuality is normal. These individuals do not eschew sex because of traumatic experiences, they are not horny people who chose a life of celibacy, they just don't feel the urge to merge. Interestingly, in fact, it is useful to think about sexual orientation from two angles, one is from heterosexual to homosexual, the other is amount of desire from constantly horny to asexual.

Sex Summary

So, what does all of this mean? First, sex is important—in fact, what we think of ourselves as a sexual person directly correlates with how we think of ourselves as human beings. Sexuality plays a significant role in our self-esteem and emotional well-being. It is important to realize that no two people are the same, so there is no such thing as normal. What is right for two people in a relationship is what works for them. Feeling safe to completely let go—both physically and emotionally—with a partner has a powerful bonding effect.

Okay, now that we have gotten to know each other better, had dinner and then sex, it is time to take this tour into a dark, mysterious neighborhood of humanity. Buckle your safety belts as we sink into your fears . . .

Terms of Endearment: Definitions of What We Do

You name it. Someone is having sex with it. Check the boxes of the activities that interest you, then share the list with your partner. Use this list to explore your wishes.

P.S. Want to know if you are crazy? If you checked "allorgasmia" before giving this list to your partner, then yes, you are crazy.

Acousticophilia	Sexual arousal from particular sounds	❑
Acrotomophilia	Sexual arousal by the activity/thought of having sex with an amputee	❑
Agalmatophilia	A fetish, sexual arousal for statues/ mannequins	❑
Agoraphilia	Arousal from having sex in public places	❑
Agrexophilia	Excitement from knowing that others are aware of a person's sexual activities	❑
Albutophilia	Arousal from water	❑

Allorgasmia	The need to fantasize about a more desirable partner in order to orgasm	❑
Amelotasis	Attraction to someone who has lost a limb	❑
Analingus	Any act of oral stimulation to the anus or perianal areas, also referred to as rimming	❑
Automysophilia	Sexual arousal from being dirty or defiled	❑
Axillism	Using the armpit for sex (as a substitute vagina)	❑
Bestiality	Having sexual contact with an animal	❑
Bondage	Sexual practice of physically restraining another	❑
Choreophilia	Sexual arousal from dancing	❑
Coprophilia	Sexual arousal from feces	❑
Cunnilingus	Any act of oral stimulation of the vulva or clitoris	❑
Doraphilia	Love of fur or animal skin (usually leather)	❑
Emetophilia	Arousal from vomit or vomiting	❑
Erotographomania	Strong desire to write love letters or poetry	❑
Exhibitionism	Sexual arousal by exposing genitals to an unsuspecting stranger, usually in inappropriate settings	❑

Fetishism	Sexual arousal by using or thinking about an inanimate object or the viewing of a particular part of the body	❑
Flatuphilia	Arousal from others passing gas	❑
Frotteurism	Sexual arousal and gratification by rubbing one's genitals against others in public places or crowds	❑
Gomphipothic	Arousal from the sight of teeth	❑
Hypersexuality	Intense and compulsive sex drive with little or no sexual gratification despite numerous partners	❑
Kleptophilia	Sexually aroused and gratified by the act of stealing, or aroused by the danger of being caught stealing	❑
Klismaphilia	Sexual arousal and gratification by being given an enema	❑
Knismolagnia	Arousal from tickling	❑
Masochism	Sexual arousal and gratification by having pain inflicted upon oneself	❑
Mixoscopy	The observation of a sex act in secret (see voyeurism)	❑
Mysophilia	The arousal from handling soiled underwear, foul odors, or filthy surroundings	❑
Nymphomania	The term for women experiencing hypersexuality	❑

Ochlophilia	Bite me . . . oh, I mean arousal from biting	❏
Philemanmania	Compulsion to kiss	❏
Phobophilia	Sexual arousal from fear	❏
Podophilia	Foot fetish	❏
Sadism	Sexual arousal and gratification by the act of inflicting pain on another person	❏
Satyriasis	The term for men experiencing hypersexuality	❏
Stigmatophilia	Sexual arousal and gratification by marking one's body (tattoos)	❏
Transvestism	Sexual arousal or gratification from dressing in the clothes of the opposite sex	❏
Troilism	Sexual arousal and gratification by sharing a sexual partner while watching. A troilist becomes aroused and gratified by the "sharing"	❏
Urophilia	"Golden showers" or "water sports"; Sexual arousal and gratification through urinating or watching the act of urination	❏
Voyeurism	"Peeping Tomism"; sexual arousal and gratification by observing nude individuals without their knowledge or consent	❏

Pyrophilia	Sexually aroused and gratified watching and/or setting fires, or from the heat of a fire	❏
Sotophilia	Sexual arousal by the sight of certain foods	❏
Tantalolagnia	Sexual arousal from teasing	❏
Tripsolagnia	Sexual arousal from having one's hair shampooed by another	❏
Zelophilia	Sexual arousal from jealousy	❏
Zoophilia	The stroking or petting of an animal as an erotic stimulus	❏

5.

scared silly: fears and phobias

There are times when fear is good. It must keep its watchful place at the heart's controls. There is advantage in the wisdom won from pain.

—AESCHYLUS, GREEK DRAMATIST, 450 BCE

You have every reason to be afraid. It's your birthright. You need to be afraid. Without real, honest-to-goodness fear, your instinct for self-preservation would vanish. It has kept our species alive in a dangerous world. Those who lacked the primordial emotion have ejected themselves from the gene pool. In other words, the reckless and the fearless tend to die young. Once an individual has a family, the instinct for self-preservation extends to family members. Beyond merely having children, we must protect them at all costs.

Whenever we are in a fearful situation, our brains record all the details for future reference. After suffering a dog bite, you might find yourself experiencing dread every time you see a dog. That's a learned fear, acquired through the experience of a traumatic event. As the saying goes, "Once bitten, twice shy." A fear

Fear triggers our fight-or-flight response.

may also be learned through others. If mother is afraid of cats, there must be a good reason to fear them. While many fears are learned, others are innate, including a fear of loud noises, heights, snakes, and spiders. Without biologically determined fears, we'd think spiders were fuzzy play toys and jumping off cliffs was liberating.

Fear is the catalyst that triggers our fight-or-flight response. When we sense an imminent threat, our bodies prepare for danger. We experience increased heart rate, dilated pupils, rapid breathing, increased sweating, and tense or trembling muscles. These responses exist for a reason. On the surface, the fight-or-flight instinct is contradictory, signaling offense and defense. But this is good, as either option may be necessary for survival. A racing heart and rapid breathing floods our bodies with oxygen, preparing us to fight for our lives or flee as fast as we can to avoid injury. Sweating cools the body, but also makes us slippery and harder to grasp. Paralyzing fear, the type that holds us motionless, dates back to our hunter-gatherer days when any motion might have drawn the attention of a nearby predator. Even fainting had a purpose—it served as a playing dead response to create disinterest in some predators.

While the involuntary scream might scare off startled predators, the sound also serves as a distress call to rally tribe members. What is our first instinct when we hear someone scream? Focus on that person and investigate—cautiously. Ever wonder why our hair stands on end when we're afraid? This response dates back to when humans had hairier pelts. It bristled, and made our ancestors appear larger, more imposing. Has fear ever made you cold? If it has, you weren't imagining the reaction. When we're afraid, the blood vessels constrict in order to minimize bleeding in the event of injury. Without that full flow of blood, we feel the full chill of fear.

Our physiological responses to fear can also lead to gut-wrenching turmoil. When we are extremely afraid, our bodies focus on safety and waste no energy on digestion. The digestive and urinary systems empty by whatever means necessary. In modern society, stressful situations and performance anxiety such as the night before a difficult meeting or presentation are likely to trigger troublesome digestive-system responses.

Because we no longer hide in caves or climb trees to elude predators, our reservations have become less dire. Once, we feared for our lives on a regular basis; now we fear poor job-performance reviews. In the past, we worried about finding shelter and enough food to eat; now we worry about high insurance rates. Though there are times when some face grave danger, most of us manage to get through years without encountering a true life-and-death emergency. Yet, fear is too important to the survival of our species for it to atrophy.

As young children, we discover that fear can be fun. Campfire ghost stories, haunted houses, and roller coaster rides use fear to generate exhilaration. By experiencing the excitement without true risk, some of us become adrenaline junkies. We seek out scary movies or horror novels to scratch the fear itch. The adrenaline rush generated by these fears lifts us out of the doldrums of everyday civilized life. This may be nature's way of keeping our fear response in tune.

DO YOU HAVE A PHOBIA?

According to psychiatrists, if you answer "yes" to all of the following questions, you have a phobia.

1. Are you irrationally or excessively scared of a situation, creature, or object?

2. Are you far more afraid of the situation, creature, or object than you should be?

3. Do you avoid or loathe encountering the situation, creature, or object?

4. Do you immediately experience extreme anxiety when exposed to the situation, creature, or object?

5. Does your fear interfere with your life?

A Scare to Remember

The human mind uses our memories of the past to plan for the future. But what happens when our recollections of healthy fears generalize and become anxiety disorders that cause us to retreat into our homes, afraid to step out into the world? While someone with too little fear may be unceremoniously removed from the gene pool, one with too much fear may never hop in. Our fight-or-flight instinct, designed to protect us, can go wrong and imprison us.

Fear or Phobia

Almost one in every five Americans develops chronic or unrealistic fears. These phobias cause overwhelming distress and reduce the ability to function in society. Many more people describe themselves as phobics but are nothing of the sort, at least not in the clinical sense. While you may be apprehensive about rush-hour driving or worry about clicking the wrong buttons on a computer screen, that doesn't mean you have a phobia. A phobic reaction is not one of distaste or aversion, but rather of terror that is out of proportion to the threat.

Circle a number from the scale below that best represents how much you would avoid each of the situations listed because of fear or other unpleasant feelings.

	Would Not Avoid It		Slightly Avoid It	Definitely Avoid It		Markedly Avoid It		Always Avoid It
1. Walking alone on busy streets	0	1	2	3	4	5	6	7	8
2. Injections or minor surgery	0	1	2	3	4	5	6	7	8
3. Eating or drinking with other people	0	1	2	3	4	5	6	7	8
4. Traveling alone by bus or train	0	1	2	3	4	5	6	7	8
5. Hospitals	0	1	2	3	4	5	6	7	8
6. Being watched or stared at	0	1	2	3	4	5	6	7	8
7. Going into crowded shops	0	1	2	3	4	5	6	7	8
8. The sight of blood	0	1	2	3	4	5	6	7	8
9. Talking to people in authority	0	1	2	3	4	5	6	7	8
10. Going alone far from home	0	1	2	3	4	5	6	7	8
11. The thought of injury or illness	0	1	2	3	4	5	6	7	8
12. Speaking or acting to an audience	0	1	2	3	4	5	6	7	8
13. Large open spaces	0	1	2	3	4	5	6	7	8
14. Going to the dentist	0	1	2	3	4	5	6	7	8
15. Being criticized	0	1	2	3	4	5	6	7	8

Adapted from Marks, I.M. and Mathews, A.M. (1978) Brief Standard Self-rating for Phobic Patients. Behavior Research and Therapy, 17, 263–267. Used by permission.

Scoring Your Test

This is one of those delightfully sneaky tests that measure several aspects of your personality. This test provides insight in to three separate types of fears. To calculate your scores, add up your answers to the following sets of five questions:

Agoraphobia
Q1_____
Q4_____
Q7_____
Q10_____
Q13_____
Your Score:_____

Blood/Injury
Q2_____
Q5_____
Q8_____
Q11_____
Q14_____
Your Score:_____

Social Fears
Q3_____
Q6_____
Q9_____
Q12_____
Q15_____
Your Score:_____

Agoraphobia

While many people think agoraphobia is the fear of open spaces, this set of fears is more complex. Agoraphobia is a marked fear of being in a situation from which you cannot easily escape. People who score high in this category fear losing control or that something embarrassing will happen to them when they are surrounded by other people. Think of being in a crowded classroom, meeting, or restaurant, and fainting, not being able to breathe, or losing control of your bladder. Sure, these things are unlikely, but to the agoraphobic, it is not worth taking the chance. People with agoraphobia avoid situations where they would be unable to leave quickly if something embarrassing happened to them.

Blood and Injury

The fear of illness and injury is probably one of the easiest fears to understand. Most of us do not relish the thought of sickness or physical impairment; nor do we look forward to hospital food, injections, or the taste of medicine. We all have an elderly relative who, although really ill, refuses to go to the doctor, or know someone who fears that she has cancer, although she has no symptoms. Living through painful experiences and hearing the traumatic incidents of others may result in a lifelong fear.

Social Fears

For psychologists, these are the fascinating ones. Social phobia is the dread of being watched, criticized, or humiliated while doing something social. The most common example is the fear of being in front of an audience to give a speech or performance. But other situations include routine activities such as being frightened to eat a meal near strangers, write a check at the grocery store, or even having sex. Mild cases create "butterflies" in the stomach and tension, but those who get higher scores on this category know the great lengths they will go through to avoid social situations.

WHAT DOES YOUR SCORE MEAN?

The range of possible scores in each subtest is from zero to forty. The higher your score, the greater your fears. While there is not a formal threshold score for being labeled as fearful, you can see that by the time scores climb above twelve or so, phobias are beginning to impact behavior.

Score of 0 to 12—Cool Cucumber

There isn't much that bothers you or that you can't handle. You take things in stride and have an air of confidence. You generally feel competent and believe you can handle most stressful situations with aplomb. Life may throw you curveballs now and then, but you always adjust your swing and get on base.

Score of 13 to 20—Tense Times

You are troubled by some situations where you feel a loss of control. You prefer the routine to the unexpected. You recognize that you have some fears and adjust your behavior somewhat to feel more comfortable. Usually, you can deal with your peccadilloes and get through the day. If you feel that the balance in your life is becoming precarious, talking to a therapist may help you prune those unreasonable fears before they grow too large.

Score of Above 20—Frequently Fearful

You are riddled with unproductive phobias and have trouble reaching the full quality of your life. The unexpected makes you uncomfortable, and your concerns interfere with your enjoyment of life and may keep you housebound and unnecessarily anxious. A therapist may be able to help you regain control so you can spend less time worrying about life and more time enjoying it.

Simple Phobias

Now that we know a little more about broad types of fears, we are going to slice them up into simple phobias and complex ones. Simple or specific phobias refer to fears of particular objects or situations. Common specific phobias include fears of snakes, spiders, mice, and dogs, but also situations like tall heights and flying.

ANIMAL FEARS

A fear of snakes certainly seems understandable, even culturally acceptable. Not only are snakes a physical threat (sharp fangs, strike suddenly, sometimes poisonous), but they have been portrayed as evil in literature, folklore and religion. (Who tempted Eve in the Garden of Eden?) We can visualize a woman leaping onto a kitchen chair and shrieking the moment she spies a mouse. But is that a learned fear through transference? After all, mice aren't physically threatening. Or do we realize on a deeper level that rodents invade our foodstuffs and carry disease? After all, rats were responsible for spreading the plague and wiping out vast numbers of the human race. It may surprise you to learn that many people are afraid of another member of the animal kingdom, most commonly referred to as man's best friend: dogs.

When Gracie was three years old, riding her tricycle along her driveway, the neighbor's Rottweiler jumped over the fence and knocked her to the ground. The dog then chased her all the way to the front door of her house. While Gracie sustained no physical wounds, the incident left psychological scars. Grace is now thirty-three years old and is deathly afraid of dogs. Whenever she sees a dog approach, her heart begins to beat fast, her mouth becomes dry, and she crosses the street to avoid contact. The dog's size and demeanor do not matter—Grace is afraid of and hates all dogs. She has generalized from one traumatic episode to all dogs for thirty years—and counting.

FORCES OF NATURE

Scary books and films often use thunderstorms to help set a dark mood, creating a sense of danger and anxiety. We're all familiar with the scene of a woman alone in a creepy, old house. Cue the thunder and lightning. The lights go dark. Oh no! What happens next . . . ?

It seems natural to fear nature's fury. Thunderstorms rage across the sky with loud bangs, sudden flashes of light in the roiling darkness shake the earth. Tornadoes and hurricanes wreak havoc wherever they strike, destroying homes and killing people indiscriminately. Raw power, death, and destruction are good reasons for a healthy dose of fear. Yet, some people have natural fears so unusual it's hard to rationalize them. Would it surprise you to learn that some people fear simpler elements of life on earth like the moon and stars?

For example, Tammy suffers with onbrophobia—she has an excessive and persistent fear of rain. Tammy knows her phobia is kind of silly. She gets embarrassed when asked to discuss it. But her ombrophobia is very real. Tammy will not leave her home if there is rain in the forecast. One time last year, a storm suddenly sprung up while she was at the movies. Tammy did not realize it was raining until she was about to leave. When she saw wet clusters of patrons waiting under shelter for the rain to stop, her mouth went dry, her palms started sweating, and she could not speak or think clearly. She felt she was losing control of her mind. Thankfully, Tammy's date immediately recognized what was happening and guided her into another show until the storm passed.

Onbrophobia: the excessive and persistent fear of rain

ON SECOND THOUGHT, MAYBE YOU SHOULD BE AFRAID!

Most of us assume the best place to combat illness and return to health is in a hospital. But those who suffer from nosocomephobia, the fear of hospitals, may have good cause for their contrary perspective. Each year, more than two million people pick up an infection while they are in the hospital. Stethoscopes, blood-pressure cuffs, blankets, and even hospital walls are breeding grounds for bacteria. Surprisingly, one of the most common ways that bacteria spread to patients is from health care workers who neglect to wash their hands.

Having a fear of the color red (erythrophobia) seems downright odd, wouldn't you say? But did you know that by eating a cherry Popsicle you could be consuming bits of bug? Or, ladies, that you could be smearing bug guts on your lips along with that vibrant red lipstick you like to wear? Cochineals, beetles harvested in Peru, are used as a natural way to color food and cosmetics. The cochineal, which is the size of a tick, is the only bug the FDA has approved for human consumption. Next time you pop a stick of grape-flavored gum in your mouth or eat strawberry yogurt, think about this tiny bug and ping your fear.

Ailurophobia, the fear of cats, seems a bit more unexpected than fear of dogs, until you learn that a skin-breaking scratch from a cat can cause a serious infection resulting in a high fever and swollen lymph nodes. Even bites from cats are more dangerous than those from dogs—the puncture wounds are deeper and there is a 40 percent greater chance of infection.

A peaceful, secluded lake seems like the perfect spot for a relaxing summer vacation, as long as you don't have limnophobia, a fear of lakes. But that fear might not be such a bad thing. Lakes are not regulated or treated for water quality, so the water could be filled with E coli from one likely source: soiled diapers.

Moreover, lakes may be teeming with dangerous microorganisms that cause brain infections and primary amebic meningoencephalitis, a difficult-to-treat infection that can result in death within one week. Stones and tree stumps submerged beneath the surface of lakes account for many diving injuries. Think twice before you take the plunge!

Complex Phobias

We saw at the beginning of this chapter that humans are animals. We need some fears to survive in a wild world. However, we are also fundamentally social animals. Relationships, the opinions of others, and our perception of ourselves in society, are paramount to this complex creature, homo sapiens. So, apart from the simple scares of spiders and snakes, we have developed our own public panics called complex fears or social phobias.

Complex fears are designed to protect us from embarrassment. Notice that we are not talking about certain death, cuts, bruises, scrapes, or bites, but reddening of the cheeks. Our standing in our culture is so vital that many of us avoid any opportunity that might damage it—to the point of removing ourselves from society! People with a complex phobia live in a paradox. They are terrified of looking awkward or foolish, or mispronouncing a word, so they steer clear of interactions with others and situations in which these behaviors could occur.

The social fears are fascinating because they speak to the very core of what it is to be human—we are social beasts and any threat to our ability to relate to others is a tremendous danger. Isn't it odd that we can develop caligynephobia (fear of beautiful women)? Men don't grow this fear because they are afraid of getting a squirt of hairspray in the eyes or of being stabbed with a mascara wand. It is the beauty of a woman, the way it calls men to form relationships, and the fear of rejection that frighten us. We fear the siren's siren more than the serpent's fangs.

The curse of caligynephobia: the fear of beautiful women.

Those with social phobias are trapped within imaginary cages. They are their own worst critics. They imagine everyone watching them, judging them. They are so self-conscious, they monitor themselves to the point of paralysis. Social phobias are the third most common psychological disorder in the United States (right behind depression and alcoholism). Almost forty million Americans will suffer with a social phobia at some time during their lives.

DO YOU HAVE A SOCIAL PHOBIA?

Like simple fears of spiders and snakes, those with complex, social phobias behave in a particular pattern. According to psychiatrists, you have a social phobia if you answer yes to all of the following:

Are you persistently afraid of being embarrassed or humiliated in social settings or performing in public?   YES   NO

Do you feel anxious in social situations?   YES   NO

Do you recognize that your fears are excessive or unreasonable?   YES   NO

Do you try to avoid social or performance settings?   YES   NO

Does your avoidance or anxiety about these situations significantly interfere with your routine, relationships, life quality, or job?   YES   NO

XENOPHOBIA

There is one last social fear that needs to be addressed. Terrorism works when it instills fear and helplessness in people because the attacks are random, unprovoked, and, though intentional, are targeted at the defenseless. Trying to cope with the nature of terrorism causes fear, helplessness, vulnerability, and grief. One unwelcome side effect of terrorism is xenophobia—a fear or hatred of strangers or foreigners. Xenophobia is especially troubling in a diverse society like ours. It ranges from suspicion and dislike of foreigners to the extreme of committing hate crimes. It is essential to realize that strength can arise from our varied backgrounds, and it is more likely that we will find invaluable knowledge and experience to cope with terrorism from a diverse society.

When a Fear Becomes a Disorder

Let's crank things up another notch. We have been peeking in so many windows, we've forgotten the yard. Sometimes a trouble-some weed of a fear will overgrow in the garden of your mind and before you know it, your backyard has become a mess.

HAVE A CUP OF FEAR—CAFFEINE-INDUCED ANXIETY

Most people consume coffee, tea, or soda pop to fight fatigue and get an energy boost. Caffeine certainly has its way of revving up the central nervous system. Many say they cannot function until they have their first cup in the morning. And yet, for a

---

CAFFEINE INTOXICATION

While most of us know coffee can perk you up, not many realize there is a medical condition called caffeine intoxication. Quickly drinking two or three cups of coffee in a short period of time (about 250 mg of caffeine) can cause you to become intoxicated. Symptoms may include a flushed face, an upset stomach, the need to pee, agitation, as well as the warning signs for caffeine-induced anxiety.

---

small percentage of the population, caffeine causes mental distress. Caffeine-induced anxiety is the result of restlessness, nervousness, insomnia, muscle twitching, irregular heartbeat, and rambling speech. Your vulnerability to this disorder depends upon many influences such as the amount of caffeine consumed, the speed at which your body breaks down this drug, and other medical conditions which can make you especially sensitive to caffeine's effects.

DO YOU HAVE PANIC ATTACKS?

To have Panic Disorder, you must have recurring panic attacks and fear that another one could strike. According to psychiatrists, a panic attack includes at least four of the following symptoms:

A feeling of danger	Shortness of breath	The sense of things
The need to escape	Tingling sensations	being unreal
Heart palpitations	Chest pain	Fear of going crazy
Sweating	Nausea	Fear of dying
Trembling	Dizziness	Chills or hot flashes

PANIC ATTACKS AND PANIC DISORDER

A panic attack is an intense period of apprehension or terror that lasts for about ten minutes. There are three types of panic attacks:

1. **Unexpected:** The attack comes without warning and for no particular reason.

2. **Situational:** A certain situation causes the attack. For example, a person may have an attack whenever they have to drive across a bridge.

3. **Situationally Predisposed:** Situations in which a person is likely to have a panic attack, but does not always have one.

Panic attacks may also be provoked by stimulants such as caffeine, diet pills, or decongestants. These types of attacks may disappear or become less severe once the stimulant use is discontinued. Medical conditions may also cause panic attacks. Overactive thyroids, asthma, and heart arrhythmias cause the same symptoms as panic attacks.

Panic Disorder

A person diagnosed with Panic Disorder has suffered at least two panic attacks, and between episodes, is filled with anxiety, worrying when the next attack will strike.

Amanda is a pleasant, hardworking mother of two great kids. One day while at the office, Amanda suddenly felt spacey and then like the air was crushing her. For about ten minutes, she felt dizzy, short of breath, and out of control, with a sudden urge to escape. Amanda was unsure what brought on this episode, as she was just performing the routine task of filing paperwork. She hoped she would never have such an experience again. Unfortunately, while folding laundry at home a few days later, Amanda had another attack. In the coming weeks, her attacks became more frequent. And when she was not actually having an attack, Amanda was nervous about when the next one would strike. She became so preoccupied with her fear of having another attack that she couldn't concentrate. Amanda would sometimes leave her job early and run to the safety and comfort of her family. The tension grew. Some days were unbearable, and Amanda would call in sick. She felt the need to run away from these attacks and would go on frequent walks. Amanda had trouble sleeping, which was especially troublesome since sleep was one way she could escape the horrible feelings. She was afraid she was losing her mind. Amanda is one of the seven million Americans who develop Panic Disorder throughout their lives.

Panic Disorder can become quite disabling. It restricts the lives of sufferers—mainly women—by preventing them from performing even the most mundane of daily activities, like making trips to the bank or grocery store. Again, just like little Gracie and her run in with the Rottweiler, sufferers of panic attacks generalize and specifically avoid places where they've had a previous attack. Panic Disorder is often accompanied by other serious conditions such as depression, drug abuse, and alcoholism.

REACTING TO FRIGHT

It is important to consider that not everyone who has a panic attack will develop Panic Disorder. Many people may only experience one panic attack in their lifetime. How we react to frightening situations can help predict whether a menacing moment becomes a phobia or if a phobia develops into a disorder. This next test will help you determine how well you respond to scares.

TEST YOURSELF

Instructions

This test will help you determine how well you respond to fear. It consists of fourteen common reactions to scary situations. It only takes about five minute to complete, but there is no time limit. Think of a situation that makes you scared, then consider how frequently you exhibit each reaction. Circle the number that best represents your experiences.

Below are some thoughts that may pass through your mind when you are nervous or frightened. Please indicate how often each thought occurs when you are nervous.

	Never	Rarely	Half the Time	Usually	Always
1. I am going to throw up.	1	2	3	4	5
2. I am going to pass out.	1	2	3	4	5
3. I must have a brain tumor.	1	2	3	4	5
4. I will have a heart attack.	1	2	3	4	5
5. I will choke to death.	1	2	3	4	5
6. I am going blind.	1	2	3	4	5
7. I am going to have a stroke.	1	2	3	4	5
8. I am going to act foolish.	1	2	3	4	5
9. I will not be able to control myself.	1	2	3	4	5
10. I will hurt someone.	1	2	3	4	5
11. I am going to go crazy.	1	2	3	4	5
12. I am going to scream.	1	2	3	4	5
13. I am going to babble or talk funny.	1	2	3	4	5
14. I will be paralyzed by fear.	1	2	3	4	5

Chambless, D.L. et al. (1984) Assessment of Fear in Agoraphobics: The Body Sensations Questionnaire and the Agoraphobics Questionnaire. Journal of Consulting and Clinical Psychology, 52, 1090–1097. Used by permission.

Scoring Your Test

This is a two-pronged test that tells you a little more than you might have expected. The first half of the questions deals with the physical concerns of being afraid, while the second half uncovers your experiences with losing control. Tally your responses to questions one to seven, then eight to fourteen, and enter the results below. Your scores should be between 7 and 35 for each subtest.

Your Physical Concerns (questions 1 to 7) _____

Your Concerns over Loss of Control _____
(questions 8 to 14)

UNDERSTANDING YOUR SCORE

Your Score	Reaction to Fear
Less than 10	Cool Cat
10-12	Plucky Ducky
13-15	Indomitable Snowman
16-21	Nervous Nelly
More than 22	Scaredy Cat

WHAT DOES YOUR SCORE MEAN?
Score of Less than 12—Restrained and Graceful
Your fear response is under control. You exhibit grace under pressure and rise to the occasion in stressful situations. You weather every storm with the confidence that things will work out. Those around you appreciate your calming influence.

Score of 13 to 15—Tough and Together

You are a pretty together person. You can tough out many circumstances, but occasionally you let anxiety and stress get the better of you. Deadlines and job pressures may interfere with your ability to perform and advance in your field. Sometimes, you realize that you're acting a tad irrational, and you can keep yourself in check. You should know from experience that things won't be as bad as you fear. That extra confidence, and maybe some calming exercises, may help you retain control in stressful situations.

Score of More than 16—Scaredy Cat

It is difficult to be you when you are scared. You may remember the calming mantra "don't panic," but you are yelling it at the top of your lungs when you need it most. You let irrational behavior take control when you are afraid. Those around you may become even more stressed or alarmed because they are concerned about your reactions. Your behavior can make bad situations worse, creating self-fulfilling prophecies out of your numerous anxieties. You would be wise to seek counseling to help you deal with your reactions to fears and nervousness.

GENERALIZED ANXIETY DISORDER

Everyone worries to some extent. Normal worries are good for us. They help us focus our attention and stay motivated. Worrying about getting a speeding ticket or getting in a car accident leads us to drive safely. Fear of failing a test motivates us to study to achieve a good grade. It is when those worries interfere with our ability to handle problems effectively that we can develop Generalized Anxiety Disorder (GAD).

Casey has trouble sleeping. She has been waking up in the middle of the night feeling agitated. She has trouble concentrating during the day. Even reading a book or newspaper is difficult.

Casey is afraid her lack of attention at work will cause her to lose her job. In addition to worrying about job performance, Casey has begun to worry about her husband's safety from the moment he leaves in the morning until he returns in the evening. Casey fears her husband will die, and she finds it hard to rid herself of these thoughts. Though her stress is responsible for her fatigue, headaches, stomachaches, and irritability, she fears these physical ailments are symptoms of a terrible disease that will certainly result in her death. Casey has Generalized Anxiety Disorder.

GAD often strikes in childhood or adolescence, but can begin in adulthood. The disorder occurs gradually and a person is diagnosed with GAD when she spends at least six months excessively worrying about everyday problems. Though the person with GAD knows her worries are unfounded, she finds it impossible to shake off those concerns. GAD affects more women than men, and may run in families. Often, people with GAD will say things like "I'm just like my mother" or "Dad was the same way." The disorder is usually accompanied by depression, substance abuse, or other anxiety disorders. The most common treatment is using medications.

The Only Thing We Have to Fear . . .

We have covered a lot of ground in this part of the tour. We have peeked into the dark recesses of fears, terror, and anxiety. We have probed behavior that upsets many of us and have even looked into how we react when we're scared. Remember, it is natural to have some fear. Only a fool would not be afraid of a charging bull or a tornado two blocks away. The adrenaline rush before performing on stage actually aids the actors in doing their best. Fears only become phobias when they start to affect our lives in negative ways.

DO YOU HAVE GENERAL ANXIETY DISORDER?

You have General Anxiety Disorder if you answer yes to these three questions:

1. Do you worry excessively about all sorts of things and find it difficult to control your worrying?   YES   NO

2. Have you been troubled like this on most days for the past six months?   YES   NO

3. Do you have at least three of the following symptoms?   YES   NO

Feeling restless or on edge	Irritability
Tire easily	Muscle tension
Trouble concentrating	Trouble sleeping

I hope this chapter has given you further insights into what life is like for those who live with phobias. Because of our genes and personal experiences, no two people have the same fears. In fact, there are enough terms for fears to create a dictionary. We finish this chapter with a list of the more quirky phobias. Not only are the words kind of fun to figure out, but thinking about how and why we develop each of these is a treat.

Your Glossary of Quirky Phobias

Ablutophobia— Fear of washing or bathing
Alektorophobia— Fear of chickens
Allodoxaphobia— Fear of opinions
Anginophobia— Fear of sore throats
Anthophobia— Fear of flowers

Apotemnophobia— Fear of amputees

Arachibutryophobia— Fear of peanut butter sticking to the roof of your mouth (I'm not kidding)

Automatonophobia— Fear of ventriloquist's dummies

Bibliophobia— Fear of books

Bogyphobia— Fear of demons and goblins

Cacophobia— Fear of ugliness

Caligynephobia— Fear of beautiful women

Cathisophobia— Fear of sitting down

Chinophobia— Fear of snow

Chorophobia— Fear of dancing

Cibophobia— Fear of food

Coitophobia— Fear of having sexual intercourse

Cyberphobia— Fear of computers

Anthophobia—the fear of flowers.

Dishabiliophobia— Fear of undressing in front of others

Enosiophobia— Fear of having committed an unpardonable sin

Eosophobia— Fear of dawn or daylight

Euphobia— Fear of hearing good news

Genuphobia— Fear of knees

Graphophobia— Fear of writing or handwriting

Hippopotomonstrosesquippedaliophobia— Fear of long words!

Hobophobia— Fear of the destitute

Homilophobia— Fear of sermons

Hygrophobia— Fear of liquids, dampness or moisture

Kosmikophobia— Fear of cosmic phenomena

Listophobia— Fear of lists

Limnophobia— Fear of lakes

Liticaphobia— Fear of lawsuits

Melophobia— Fear or hatred of music

Metrophobia— Fear or hatred of poetry

Mnemophobia— Fear of memories

Myrmecophobia— Fear of ants

Nephophobia— Fear of clouds (well, they can form some fairly scary shapes!)

Nomatophobia— Fear of names

Nosocomephobia— Fear of hospitals

Novercaphobia— Fear of your mother-in-law

Panophobia— Fear of everything

Peladophobia— Fear of bald people

Philemaphobia— Fear of kissing

Phobophobia— Fear of fear

Politicophobia— Fear or dislike of politicians

Proctophobia— Fear of rectum or rectal diseases

Pteronophobia— Fear of being tickled by feathers

Teratophobia— Fear of giving birth to monsters

Theatrophobia— Fear of theatres

Tremophobia— Fear of trembling

Triskaidekaphobia— Fear of the number 13

Venerophobia— Fear of venereal disease

Vestiphobia— Fear of clothing

Wiccaphobia— Fear of witches and witchcraft

Xerophobia— Fear of dryness

Xenophobia— Fear or hatred of strangers or foreigners

Xylophobia— Fear of wooden objects, even forests

Zeusophobia— Fear of gods

Zoophobia— Fear of animals

6.

weird shit: obsessions, compulsions, and more bizarre behaviors

There is a bunch of weird shit in this book.

—EDITOR REVIEWING THIS MANUSCRIPT

Okay, we are going to call it as we see it. This chapter deals with weird shit—the bizarre behavior that appeals to our gruesome sense of curiosity. It is like stumbling upon a car accident and not being able to turn away. These disorders are rare, but very real. Be prepared for some truly strange sightings as we journey down the winding road of exceptional personalities. First stop: Prosopagnosia.

Facing Facts: Prosopagnosia

Can you imagine looking into your loved one's faces and see-ing . . . nothing? Going up to your daughter and asking, "Don't I know you?" People suffering from prosopagnosia, or face blindness, have difficulty recognizing people by their faces. This includes the faces of close friends, family members—even their own! They must rely on nonfacial cues for recognition, such as hair, voice, and clothing. To someone with face blindness, faces look as varied to them as rocks look different to us.

It is easier for prosopagnosics to recognize faces if they are upside down.

Imagine you pick up a handful of gravel and look at each little stone. Although they each have various pits and striations, their differences are not immediately apparent. Then, imagine this is how your family and friends look to you. Imagine trying to meet people, follow the plot of a television show, or interact at work each day. There is no treatment for this disorder which affects about one in fifty, although remarkably, it is easier for prosopagnosics to recognize faces if they are upside down.

Encopresis

There couldn't be a chapter on weird shit without a description of encopresis. Thankfully, this is a condition much more common in children than adults, but adults who have this . . . well . . . let's put it this way, encopresis is the frequent intentional or accidental dropping of feces in inappropriate places. Yes, there is enuresis too. Hmmm, okay, let's quickly move this tour along. Come on, let's see some movement.

Impulse Control Disorder

Say you wanted to do something over and over again. Anything. Eat a slice of pizza, dance around naked, or pat strangers on the top of their heads. Think of that wish, then pretend that there is nothing you can do from stopping yourself. You are compelled to do that activity. The temptation is overwhelming. A person with Impulse Control Disorder is compelled to do something and has lost control of the compulsion. There are many subdivisions of this disorder, so let's take a peek into the homes of a few of them.

SPLITTING HAIRS: TRICHOTILLOMANIA

Trichotillomania is irresistible hair pulling. It used to be considered rare, but university studies suggest that perhaps two million Americans will suffer with this disorder at some point in their lives. The need to pull a hair increases. You resist it, tension grows. Finally, the only relief is to pull hairs—mostly one at a time, often eye lashes and brows, but any body hair is fair game.

When Morgan was nine, a friend of hers wanted a pony badly. Soooo badly. Morgan's friend begged, pleaded, and pouted to her parents, but to no avail. One day at school, Morgan's friend had an inspiration. She would make a special eyelash wish and finally get her foal. After several painful attempts, Morgan's friend pulled out a lash, held it on her finger, closed her eyes, and made a wish for that horse. Then it was Morgan's turn. She struggled for a moment, then pulled out an eyelash. At that moment, something clicked in Morgan's brain. She felt a tremendous sense of relief. The problems of her weird Mom and distant Dad vanished.

Later, she referred to the sensation like enjoying her first orgasm. Although not a sexual feeling, it felt great, and for a few minutes, her troubles were gone. At that moment, Morgan's trichotillomania began. Within two days, Morgan had pulled out every eyelash and eyebrow. Her cute little face went from angelic to bald. Morgan is in her thirties now with three children. She still suffers with bouts of enthusias-

Trichotillomania: Enthusiastic hair-pulling

tic hair pulling. Keeping her hair cut short helps. On a good day, Morgan will only yank three hairs.

DO YOU HAVE TRICHOTILLOMANIA?

It is normal for people to twist their hair, pick at body parts, or even pull out the occasional body hair when bored or under stress. However, you are considered to have trichotillomania if you answer "yes" to these four questions.

Do you have a recurring pattern of pulling out your hair that results in visible hair loss?   YES   NO

Do you have an increased sense of tension immediately before pulling out a hair?   YES   NO

When you pull a hair, do you get a sense of pleasure or gratification?   YES   NO

Does this habit cause you distress, impair your relationships, or affect your employment?   YES   NO

BURNING DESIRES: PYROMANIA

Most fires attributable to arson are started for financial reasons (collecting insurance), to hide evidence of a crime, to show anger, as a political statement or terrorist act, or in response to a hallucination or delusion. People with pyromania, however, do not set fires for any of the above reasons. Pyromaniacs—who tend to be adolescent or young adult males—set fires because of an unnatural impulse—they love fires. They are fascinated with fire and anything associated with fires (fire engines, fire stations, fire-fighting equipment). Like a person with trichotillomania, they grow tense up to the moment they set the fire, but experience pleasure and relief as they set it and watch it burn. Interestingly, after the fire, pyromaniacs feel remorse, and are especially guilty if a person or animal is harmed. Because these people cannot resist the persistent, recurring nature of their love, a pyromaniac may set hundreds of fires.

STOLEN MOMENTS: KLEPTOMANIA

Stealing is common among most animal species. We steal because we want to gain something we don't have. When American outlaw Willie Sutton was asked why he robbed banks, his answer was simple: "Because that is where the money is." A person with kleptomania thinks a little differently about theft.

Kathie was the daughter of a wealthy businessman who provided her with a substantial allowance. Rarely denied anything she needed or wanted, Kathie often went out shopping on Saturdays. One day, with plenty of money and several charge cards in her purse, Kathie visited the local shopping mall and came home with a stolen pair of earrings worth $9.99 hidden in her pocket. Kathie had no idea why she would pilfer the earrings, which were well within her means and not really her style anyway. All she knew was that by the time she came home with the cheap earrings, the thrill had worn off.

ARE YOU A KLEPTOMANIAC?

While most people have pilfered a pack of gum or a candy bar sometime during their childhood, you are considered to have kleptomania if you answer "yes" to these three questions.

Do you have a recurring failure to resist impulses to steal objects that you do not need or plan to sell?   YES   NO

Do you have an increased sense of tension immediately before committing the theft?   YES   NO

Once you have committed the theft, do you get a sense of pleasure or gratification?   YES   NO

Do you steal for reasons other than anger or vengeance?   YES   NO

But then it started again—the urge to take something. The impulse called to her. She'd go out "shopping" alone. Like many kleptomaniacs, certain stores fed that urge for Kathie. She had triggers. The smell of the perfume counter made her mind writhe with need. She had no plan, no need for cheap trinkets. She needed the release stealing provided. The impulse kept her pocketing junk and hating herself afterward. Like most kleptomaniacs, Kathie did not seek treatment until she was caught.

BIG BOMB/SHORT FUSE: INTERMITTENT EXPLOSIVE DISORDER

Most people know Dennis as an easy-going, mild-mannered person. Dennis is the coach of the local girl's basketball team and takes great pride in his team victories. At practice one day, one of the girls misses a free throw. Unexpectedly, Dennis grabs a ball and heaves it at the young girl, yelling at her incompetence for missing the shot. A few moments later, Dennis feels horrified over his outburst.

People with Intermittent Explosive Disorder (IED) experience unwanted episodes of violent and aggressive behavior that may cause harm to others or destroy property. Generally, those with IED—usually men—are timid and quiet people, until they erupt in uncharacteristically violent behavior. These attacks come on suddenly and are followed by feelings of shame and remorse. Usually family members, coworkers, and friends are the victims of this aggressive behavior.

How Impulsive Are You?

In addition to impulsions like hair pulling, stealing, and fire starting, there are skin pullers and nail biters, impulsive workers (workaholics), and gamblers. The irresistible urge to do things can be extremely enticing. The buildup, then sudden rush of excitement, is seductive. Let's stop the tour for a moment and see how impulsive you are.

TEST YOURSELF

Instructions

Dr. Ernest Barratt, a professor of psychiatry at the Univerity of Texas, knows about impulsive behavior. He has spent his career trying to detangle the complex nature of these disorders and has published over 100 scientific papers sharing his findings with the international community. Dr. Barrett developed an impulsivity test that is used around the world. He has granted permission to include his test in this book provided readers are reminded that this test, like all others presented in *Are You Crazy*? are not to be used for diagnostic purposes. These tests are here to provide you with insight and understanding. If you believe you may have an emotional, psychological, or psychiatric problem, seek competent treatment from a professional.

The Barratt Impulsivity Scale lists twenty-two behaviors. All you have to do is circle the number that best represents how frequently you engage in each one.

HOW IMPULSIVE ARE YOU?

Circle the number that best represents your behavior.

	Rarely/Never	Occasionally	Often	Almost Always
1. I plan tasks carefully.	4	3	2	1
2. I am self-controlled.	4	3	2	1
3. I save regularly.	4	3	2	1
4. I am a careful thinker.	4	3	2	1
5. I plan for job security.	4	3	2	1
6. I say things without thinking.	1	2	3	4
7. I like to think about complex problems.	4	3	2	1
8. I plan trips well ahead of time.	4	3	2	1
9. I get easily bored when solving thought problems.	1	2	3	4
10. I am more interested in the present than in the future.	1	2	3	4
11. I like puzzles.	4	3	2	1
12. I do things without thinking.	1	2	3	4
13. I make up my mind quickly.	1	2	3	4
14. I am happy-go-lucky.	1	2	3	4
15. I change jobs.	1	2	3	4
16. I act on impulse.	1	2	3	4
17. I act on the spur of the moment.	1	2	3	4

	Rarely/Never	Occasionally	Often	Almost Always
18. I change where I live.	1	2	3	4
19. I buy things on impulse.	1	2	3	4
20. I can only think about one problem at a time.	1	2	3	4
21. I spend or charge more than I earn.	1	2	3	4
22. I am future-oriented.	4	3	2	1

Barratt, Earnest S. (1995). The Barratt Impulsiveness Scale, Version 11, Nonplanning and Motor Impulsiveness. Subtests Used by permission.

Scoring Your Test

This clever test has two parts: lack of planning and motor impulsiveness. Lack of planning measures forethought and consideration of consequences, while motor impulsiveness focuses on acting without thinking.

To learn your scores simply add the numbers you circled in each of the following questions:

Your Lack of Planning (questions 1 to 11) _____

Your Motor Impulsiveness (questions 12 to 22) _____

UNDERSTANDING YOUR SCORE

LACK OF PLANNING

Your Score	Percentile	Level of Planning
21 or less	15	Planned
24	30	Prepared
27	50	Primed
30	70	Improvised
33 or more	85	Impromptu

WHAT DOES YOUR SCORE MEAN?

Score of Less than 25—Planner

You are that wonderful meticulous, disciplined, almost fussy type of person that employers love. But there is a problem—sometimes you get so caught up in the details of tasks that you lose sight of the big picture. Sometimes, you forget to have fun. Life can be trying for you when the unexpected happens and you have to alter your course. So, while you are splendid at weighing the pros and cons and coming up with thoughtful decisions, try to enjoy a little spontaneity along the way—after all, it is one of the pleasures of life.

Score of 25 to 30—Well-Balanced

Good score! Your results indicate that you achieve a healthy balance between carefully thinking out your next move and enjoying some spontaneity. You are someone who can see the big picture *and* the details. Consequently, when there is a need for flexibility and quick action, you are ready.

Score of Over 30—Spur-of-the-Moment

Who needs details!? You don't get caught up with minutia. To you, life is for living not planning. Preparation, discussion, and meetings bore you silly. You go with your gut, and it seldom lets you down. While you are a fun, spontaneous person, you can drive others crazy with your lack of plans. How do they know what you want to do tonight? How can they set up the weekend? If your partner or friends score lower than 30 on this test, you should consider their needs for details and plans.

MOTOR IMPULSIVITY

Your Score	Percentile	Level of Impulsivity
17 or less	15	Stoic
19	30	Structured
21	50	Spontaneous
23	70	Impulsive
25 or more	85	Imprudent

WHAT DOES YOUR SCORE MEAN?

Score of Less than 20—Deliberate by Design

You make lists, you follow directions, and you never leave home without wearing clean underwear, just in case you're in an accident. When going on trips, you are most comfortable when you have your checklist complete, reservations in hand, and the tank full of gas. People love you at work because you always know what is next on the agenda, and your coworkers can rely on you to be there and ready. The problem is, sometimes others will see you as a little too staid, stolid, and serious. Your friends may long to see a little spontaneity. If you want this too, go ahead, be a little impulsive. But remember, planning impulsive acts doesn't count!

Score of 20 to 23—Occasionally Frivolous

Terrific test result! You are quite capable of weighing the pros and cons of an issue, then letting loose and doing what tickles your fancy instead. You have good balance in this personality trait. You are a fun friend, because while your pals can rely on you, sometimes your wild streak kicks in and surprises them.

Score of Over 24—Impulsive and Rash
I'm afraid to give you your test result because you are likely to fling the book out the window! You are impulsive with a wild side that goes all the way around. When planning a trip, all you need is the clothes on your back and the open road calling your name. Maps? Don't need them. Reservations? Too confining. Your get-up-and-go is always going. While this is a fun way to live, you may occasionally be interested in a little stability. You may find that you periodically pine for predictability. At some point, you will be ready to settle down. Until then, let your friends know that you are rash, brash, and ready to dash.

Thrill Seeking

We all know badass boys who like to squeal the tires, jump off roofs, hit golf balls at each other, and play chicken. These are the thrill seekers. Male thrill seekers tend to be more physical and many get a rush from illegal activities, while women thrillers get a greater rush from emotional daring. Do you know females who wear short skirts with nothing on underneath? Or crash a stranger's reception just to eat a piece of cake? These are the female counterparts, and while they are more subtle than the drag racers, they still fit the category of thrill seekers. The following two stories help us to identify the risk takers. As you read about them, consider where you fit in.

Samuel and Christopher drive out of town to attend a convention. They both have new cars. Sam examined safety and reliability ratings for all makes and models before deciding which car to buy. Driving in unfamiliar territory, Sam makes a note to check speed limit signs to avoid a costly speeding ticket. Chris drives the red convertible with a V-8 engine that he fell in love with on the showroom floor. Out on the highway, he bears down on the accelerator, enjoying all the power the big engine has to offer.

For his first lunch in the new city, Sam drives a few miles until he spots a national chain restaurant, where he has the same chicken dish he orders on a regular basis back home. Chris spots a small, privately owned diner and decides to try Vietnamese cuisine for the first time. That evening, Sam sits in his hotel room, reads his conference notes, and watches a familiar comedy series on television, turning in at a reasonable hour. Meanwhile, Chris asks the hotel concierge to recommend a few local hot spots for evening entertainment, and doesn't return to the hotel until well after last call.

Linda and Tanya attend the same convention. Linda packs her two best business suits that project a professional image. She places some indigestion remedies in her toiletry bag because travel usually upsets her stomach, and she wants to be prepared. Tanya is thrilled to escape the work-a-day grind. She packs the swanky designer dress she bought impulsively because it was red. Tucked away inside her suitcase are a few of the frilly undergarments she likes to wear, even under her most conservative outfits.

In the hotel bar after the meetings are over, Linda sits at a corner booth, sips a diet soda, and copies information from business cards into her daily planner. She nods politely to hotel guests who walk past her table. A few feet away, Tanya sits on a corner barstool in her low-cut dress, unwinding with a colorful cocktail as she flashes some leg. She spots a handsome man across the bar, smiles, and maintains eye contact a little longer than necessary, a bit of harmless flirting.

Unlike Sam and Linda, Chris and Tanya are thrill seekers. Sam and Linda prefer the routine, whereas Chris and Tanya are easily bored and looking for a new sensation. Scientists believe their adventurous proclivities are due to a so-called thrill-seeking gene, dubbed D4DR which, along with several other genes, seems to account for the need for speed and constant excitement. Whether or not we are thrill seekers depends on these genes and on our individual chemistry for breaking down dopamine, the natural motivator, in our brain. People with too little dopamine lack initiative, while those with too much become thrill seekers and adrenaline junkies.

While Chris and Tanya are looking for everyday thrills, excessive thrill seekers are more adventurous trying skydiving, rock climbing, white-water rafting, bungee jumping, hang gliding,

and street luge. We now have a new industry that caters to thrill-seeking athletes and their adoring fans: extreme sports.

Yet, not all thrill seekers are willing to risk life and limb for the next high. Some are more likely to risk their bank accounts and reputation instead of a broken bone. Thrill seeking accounts for many successful entrepreneurs and business executives, although many others lose the shirts off their backs.

Controversial research suggests that the same thrill-seeking genes are as likely to land you in jail as in the record books. High-sensation seekers are more willing to drive recklessly or while intoxicated, experiment with drugs, and have multiple sex partners.

A thrill is a thrill, whether it's dangerous or destructive, legal or illegal. But what triggers one thrill seeker to pursue excellence in an "X" game while another becomes addicted to heroin? Successful thrill seekers set themselves careful boundaries. They value their life, health, and family. They are optimistic. They just like to have fun in adventurous ways. Unsuccessful thrill seekers are reigned in by society and disfigurement—that is, prison and scars.

In addition, countries built through emigration, such as the United States, Canada, and Australia, tend to have a higher proportion of risk takers than other countries. Many residents of those countries have genes handed down from men and women willing to leave everything to discover and explore new frontiers.

Beyond the realm of extreme sports and stupid actions, we need thrill seekers sitting behind the steering wheels of emergency vehicles, rescuing kidnapped children, and battling fires. These people risk their lives everyday to save complete strangers. Someday we will have new worlds to explore, worlds beyond our crowded Earth. When that day comes, who do you think will be eagerly sitting atop thousands of tons of rocket fuel?

Before we leave thrill seeking, let's talk about something I like to call everyday thrills. These are the petite pick-me-ups that many of us use to add a little excitement to our days. Many of these are popular, but some are very personal. Check out the list below . . .

With a little thought, you can come up with your own personal thrills. Just try it.

Now we have reached the border and decided to cross into the risky territory called Borderline Personality Disorder. Stay close.

EVERYDAY THRILLS

You don't have to be a parachutist to enjoy a special thrill. Here is a list of modest things everyday folks do to perk up their lives. If you enjoy a little kick on occasion, try a couple of these:

- Stare at a cute stranger and hold the gaze just a little longer than usual.
- Turn up the music and dance in the house.
- Drive fast.
- Surprise your partner at work with a kiss.
- Have sex outside.
- Get a complimentary makeover.
- Sit in the dark with your friends and contemplate the universe.
- Go to a boutique just to try on fancy clothes.
- Buy fun clothes on impulse.
- Store your contact lens in the fridge for a snappy wake-up in the morning.
- Go to a restaurant and just order dessert.
- Eat free food at the grocery store.
- Exercise hard.
- Try on shoes.
- Walk around the house naked.
- Go to a car dealership to test drive a snazzy car.

Borderline Personality Disorder

Having bouts of demanding, obnoxious, or self-destructive behavior does not necessarily classify someone as having Borderline Personality Disorder. Often, other causes are to blame, including substance abuse, mood disorders, or especially difficult life circumstances. Adolescents struggling with identity issues

---

DO YOU HAVE BORDERLINE PERSONALITY DISORDER?

If you answered yes to five of these nine questions, you may be suffering from Borderline Personality Disorder.

Do you tend to have unstable, tense relationships with lots of ups and downs?	YES	NO
Do you frantically worry about being abandoned?	YES	NO
Do you have difficulty deciding who you are and what you believe?	YES	NO
Do you threaten suicide or physical harm to yourself?	YES	NO
Do you feel empty deep down inside?	YES	NO
Do your moods shift rapidly—happy one minute, sad the next?	YES	NO
Do you have difficulty controlling self-destructive impulses?	YES	NO
Do others wonder why you are so angry?	YES	NO
Under stress, do you feel detached, as if dreaming?	YES	NO

---

may experience brief periods of erratic behavior and make poor decisions regarding education and relationships. That is all part of growing up. However, much like teenagers, people with Borderline Personality Disorder experience intense joy one minute, followed by overwhelming sadness, bitterness, or anger the next. The constant shift of emotions and consequent behavior disrupt family life, work environment, and relationships with friends. They seek physical pain as a distraction from emotional pain—resorting to cutting or burning their body. Other common distractions include drug abuse, unsafe sex, reckless driving, and gambling.

While people with Borderline Personality Disorder exhibit many interesting behaviors, like extreme sarcasm and roller-coaster emotions, we are just going to pause the tour for a moment to glimpse into one of the most disturbing symptoms—self-mutilation.

SELF-MUTILATION

Kayla, a high school sophomore, has had a difficult childhood. Her father is an alcoholic who beats Kayla, her little sister, and her mother. Because of his alcoholism, Kayla's father has been fired from countless jobs, and the family has moved frequently. Kayla's mom often tells her that if she were a better child, her father would not have to beat them. Kayla feels little, if any, control over her life. She is angry with her parents and has never developed any strong friendships because of her family's repeated relocations. One night, after an argument with her parents, Kayla goes to her bedroom. She no longer knows how to deal with the anger. As a way to relieve her stress, Kayla cuts her arm with a razor blade. Oddly, this makes Kayla feel alive. For once, she feels in control. Something clicks and over the upcoming weeks, Kayla's cutting continues and eventually leads to burning her flesh with cigarettes and pulling off the dead skin.

Even though it is summer, Kayla wears long-sleeved shirts and jeans to hide the scars on her arms and legs.

Self-injury or self-mutilation—referred to as "cutting" or "si" by self-injurers—involves the deliberate damaging of body tissue without the immediate or eventual intention of committing suicide. In fact, some analysts view self-mutilation as a coping measure to *avoid* suicide. Sometimes, it is a response to abuse, becoming a form of self-abuse and a way to externalize the pain for others to see. However, sufferers are often unable to explain the reasons for their damaging behavior. Seventy-five percent of self-mutilators are female and tend to begin self-injury in adolescence.

There are three major categories of self-mutilation:

1. Superficial or moderate self-mutilation, the most common type, involves relatively minor damage, but has an addictive quality.

2. Major self-mutilation is marked by permanent disfigurement, possibly castration, or limb amputation.

3. Stereotypic self-mutilation is characterized by fixed, often rhythmic patterns, including head banging, and arm biting. This last type is seen most commonly in institutionalized or mentally challenged people.

Paranoia

As we head toward our next stop, we see a man hiding behind a bush, peeking at us. It is then that we realize that our next destination has found us—paranoia. As the old saying goes, "It is not paranoia if they are really out to get you." By implication, paranoia is the delusion—a firmly held belief that is untrue—that a nefarious "they" are out there, plotting your downfall. Conspiracy theorists have a broader concept of the mysterious "they," which may encompass the government, organized religion, secret societies, a cabal of international bankers, perhaps even anal-probe-wielding extraterrestrials. They might believe someone is

---

DO YOU HAVE PARANOID PERSONALITY DISORDER?

Paranoia is a symptom in many personality disorders. You may have paranoid personality disorder if you answer yes to four of these eight questions:

Do you think others are exploiting or tricking you?	YES	NO
Do you constantly worry about the trustworthiness of friends and coworkers?	YES	NO
Are you afraid to confide in others because they will use that information against you?	YES	NO
Do you perceive humiliating or threatening messages in innocent remarks?	YES	NO
Do you feel empty deep down inside?	YES	NO
Do you hold grudges for years and feel unable to forget past insults?	YES	NO
Do you quickly retaliate for real or imaginary criticism on your integrity?	YES	NO
Do you constantly worry that your sex partner is unfaithful?	YES	NO

---

watching them through their television or electronically eavesdropping on their phone calls. They might believe that wearing tinfoil hats will protect them against alien telepathy or mind-control rays. More often, people with paranoia find their enemies closer to home, believing their spouse is unfaithful, coworkers are making them look bad, or the boss is giving them unspectacular assignments to ruin the chance for promotion. These people may become so jealous that they spy on their spouse, eventually driving their partner away. The suspicious employees may become so obsessed with proving coworkers are undermining their job that their performance suffers and they are terminated. While the suspicions were actually unfounded, the results appear to confirm them. We can hear the rationale, "It wasn't paranoia, they were actually out to get me!"

As you can imagine, it is incredibly difficult to live with any of the symptoms above. While it takes four "yes" answers to be labeled with Paranoid Personality Disorder, just think what life is like with only one or two.

As we are being followed out of the town of Paranoia, we head to the big city where everyone knows your name—Obsessive-Compulsive Disorder.

Obsessive-Compulsive Disorder (OCD)

We all have habits and routines that are part of our lives. Routines are good. Taking the dog for a walk after dinner, humming a song while brushing your teeth, and reading a bedtime story may all be part of an established habit. Studies show that routines promote good mental and physical health; they establish a pattern of normalcy in our lives and provide us with a level of comfort.

Additionally, worries, superstitions, and rituals are common in everyday life. Some of us pray before meals, throw a pinch of salt over our shoulder, avoid stepping on cracks, chew each bite of food thirty times, genuflect in church, or check the stove and locks before leaving the house. These are common rituals that people perform every day without much thought. Some become a little peculiar. While researching this book, a friend of mine nervously disclosed that she cannot go to sleep at night until she smooths out all the wrinkles in her bedding—while she is lying in it! My daughter's teacher privately shared that she takes showers with her shoes on "so the germs don't get her."

When these rituals become excessive—hours spent washing hands or checking every lock several times—then the behavior slips into the category of Obsessive-Compulsive Disorder (OCD). The number of people who suffer from OCD has been underestimated in the past because sufferers prefer to keep their condition secret or do not seek treatment. However, according to the National Institute of Mental Health, more than three million Americans will suffer with OCD this year. OCD is an equal-opportunity ailment, striking people of all ethnic groups and affecting men and woman equally.

Obsessions are unwanted thoughts, images, or impulses that occur repeatedly and uncontrollably. Common obsessions include fear of contamination, losing control, excessive doubt (like wondering if you hit someone with your car or left a door unlocked), a need to have things "just so," and a need to tell/confess. Impulses tend to be alarming, like the desire to hurt your child or to stand up in church and swear.

In an effort to make obsessions go away, most people with OCD perform repetitive behaviors known as compulsions. It is important to realize that the compulsive behavior is the individual's attempt to gain control of the obsession. The most common obsessions are washing and checking. In an effort to rid himself from germs, a man with OCD may wash his hands until they are raw. Before leaving the house, a woman with OCD may check several times to be sure she switched off the clothes iron or locked all the windows. To make certain you don't shout cuss words, you count backwards from ten to zero—100 times!

An OCD sufferer obsessed with losing things may compulsively count them. For example, a mother may count all of her children's toys each night to make sure none of them is missing. Moreover, she may feel compelled to count the toys a set number of times each night. A man obsessed with having things orderly might have to align all the drawer handles in the house, or place the dinner dishes on the table in a certain order every night. Mentally repeating phrases and list making are also common.

TEST YOURSELF

Instructions

Do you find yourself touching the doorknob ten times before you turn it? Are you compelled to repeat a certain phrase seven times to remind yourself you turned off the stove? Is there uncertainty in your life that might seem excessive to an objective observer?

The test that follows will tell you if your quirks have passed beyond the curiosity to become a cause for concern. It is a shortened adaptation of a longer questionnaire used by psychiatrists in clinical settings. Like all tests presented in this book, this is not a diagnostic tool.

Answering the questions on this test will give you a much better idea of what it is like to have OCD. There are forty-one yes/no questions. It should take about ten minutes to complete.

HOW OBSESSED ARE YOU?

Thoughts	Yes	No
1. Are you often inwardly compelled to do certain things even though your reason tells you it is not necessary?	1	2
2. Do unpleasant or frightening thoughts or words ever keep going over and over in your mind?	1	2
3. Have you ever been troubled by certain thoughts or ideas of harming yourself or persons in your family—thoughts which come and go without any particular reason?	1	2

Checking	Yes	No
3. Do you often have to check things several times?	1	2
5. Do you ever have to check gas or water taps or light switches after you have already turned them off?	1	2
6. Do you ever have to go back and check doors, cupboards, or windows to make sure that they are really shut?	1	2

Dirt and Contamination	Yes	No
7. Do you hate dirt and dirty things?	1	2
8. Do you ever feel that if something has been used, touched, or knocked by someone else it is in some way spoiled for you?	1	2
9. Do you dislike brushing against people or being touched in any way?	1	2

Dangerous Objects	Yes	No
10. Are you ever worried by thoughts of pins, needles, or bits of hair that might have been left lying about?	1	2

Dangerous Objects

	Yes	No
11. Do you worry about household things that might chip or splinter if they were to be knocked or broken?	1	2
12. Does the sight of knives, hammers, hatchets, or other possibly dangerous things in your home ever upset you or make you feel nervous?	1	2

Personal Cleanliness and Tidiness

	Yes	No
13. Are you fussy about keeping your hands clean?		
14. Do you take care that the clothes you are wearing are always clean and neat, whatever you are doing?	1	2
15. Do you like to put your personal belongings in set places or patterns?	1	2

Household Cleanliness and Tidiness

	Yes	No
16. Do you dislike having a room untidy or not quite clean for even a short time?	1	2
17. Do your easy chairs have cushions that you like to keep exactly in position?	1	2
18. If you notice any bits or specks on the floor or furniture, do you have to remove them at once?	1	2

Order and Routine

	Yes	No
19. Do you have to keep to strict timetables or routines for doing ordinary things?	1	2
20. Do you have to keep a certain order for undressing and dressing, or washing and bathing?	1	2
21. Do you get a bit upset if you cannot do your work at set times or in a certain order?	1	2

Repetition

	Yes	No
22. Do you ever have to do things over again a certain number of times before they seem quite right?	1	2
23. Do you ever have to count things several times to go through numbers in your mind?	1	2

24. Do you ever get behind with the work because you have to do something over again several times?   1   2

Overconscientiousness and Lack of Satisfaction   Yes   No
25. Do you pay a great deal of attention to details?   1   2

---

26. Do you ever waste time by doing a thing more thoroughly than is really necessary just to see if it is really finished?   1   2

---

27. Do you feel unsettled or guilty if you haven't been able to do something exactly as you would like?   1   2

Indecision   Yes   No
28. Do you have to turn things over and over in your mind for a long time before being able to decide about what to do?   1   2

---

29. Do you ask yourself questions or have doubts about a lot of things you do?   1   2

---

30. Are there any particular things that you try to keep away from or that you avoid doing because you know that you would be upset by them?   1   2

Hoarding   Yes   No
31. Do you find it difficult to throw things away?   1   2

---

32. Do you keep a lot of empty boxes, paper bags, old newspapers, or empty tins in case they come in handy?   1   2

---

33. Does your stock of soap, detergents, or cleaning materials ever get large because you find yourself buying more than you actually use?   1   2

Stinginess   Yes   No
34. Do you get more pleasure from saving money than from spending it?   1   2

---

35. Are you more careful with money than most people you know?   1   2

---

36. Do you keep regular accounts of the money you spend every day?

	1 Yes	2 No
Irritable and Morose **37.** Do you usually look on the gloomy side of things?		
38. Do people often get on your nerves and make you feel irritable?	1	2
39. Do you get angry or irritated if people don't do things carefully or correctly?	1	2

	1 Yes	2 No
Health **40.** Do you think that regular daily bowel movements are important for your health?		
41. Do you often get scared that you might be developing some sort of serious illness or cancer?	1	2

Adapted from Cooper, J. (1970). The Leyton Obsessional Inventory, Psychological Medicine, 1(1):48–64. Used by permission.

Scoring Your Test

This test investigates fourteen dimensions of OCDs. There are only three questions for each component. Incidentally, if you noticed that the "health" component only has two questions, and that fact bothers you, you may be prone to obsessive thought.

Scoring this test is a little different from all the others. Simply review your answers for each dimension. If your answers were all "no" for a dimension, you are not obsessed in this aspect of life, move onto the next dimension. Even the occasional "yes" is no cause for alarm. Those who consistently circled two or three "yes" answers in each component should consider seeking professional help.

Earworms

Here is an obsession we all endure. Repeated sounds that relentlessly bore into our skulls. And worse, there is no known cure. You have almost certainly suffered with this condition: earworms! Otherwise known as song-stuck-in-head-syndrome. Each of us is haunted by our own demon ditties, maybe yours is the Kit-Kat candy bar jingle ("Gimme a break . . .") or that old favorite "It's a Small World After All." Most people have a personal hit parade of favorites periodically marching about their heads.

Dr. James Kellaris of the University of Cincinnati studies these rascals. He has found that nearly 98 percent of us are troubled by earworms. They irritate women significantly more than they bug men, and music lovers suffer the most. Almost two-thirds of us try to dislodge the beasts with another tune, while one in seven try to complete the song to end the suffering. In a small way, you can see that the earworm is an obsession, while completing the song is its compulsion.

SUMMARY

So here we are at the end of "weird shit." This section of our tour led us through the fascinating maze of impulse disorders. We got to meet hair pullers, fire bugs, and walking personality time bombs before moving onto thrill seekers, that lawless, no-underwear-wearing, wild crowd who, it turns out, tend to be just the type of people who founded this country. Things got a little dark with Borderline Personality and cutters, but we made it into the murky depths of paranoia, obsessions, and finally, compulsions. What a trip! Before we leave this chapter, I think it is only fair to warn you that the person who called this chapter "weird shit" referred to the next as "more weird shit."

7.

mind control: different as night and day, from dependency to sleep disorders

Emancipate yourselves from mental slavery.
None but ourselves can free our minds.　　—BOB MARLEY

We are born with free minds. Free to wander through the universe, free to create, free to love life. Then, life happens and slowly fences are erected to halt our wandering as we try to protect ourselves from hurt and pain. While some defense against the troubles of life is useful, there are those of us who build so many walls and fences that we find ourselves prisoners, only able to look up and down. Some of us carry genes that serve as fence posts—they impede mental flexibility, humor, and creativity. This chapter is about forms of control. The unusual steps we take to bolster our influence on the world, the manner in which we trick ourselves into thinking we have greater control of our worlds, and the cruel tricks our minds can play on us to usurp that precious sense of control.

Dependent Personalities

"People, people who need people are the luckiest people in the world . . ." At least, that's the way the song would have us understand it. And, for most of us, it's true. After all, we are social creatures who rely upon and delight in our relationships with others. We need others to make our way in the world—physically and emotionally. We are all familiar with the slippery slope of dependence. Few relationships lend themselves to the balance of dependence/independence like marriage. In a healthy relationship, the two partners are emotional equals and, while they may have different responsibilities, their contribution to the relationship is stable over time. To be in love begs dependence. When job stress or illness weakens our defenses, we turn to those we trust to care for us. We ask our partners how we look in outfits, what they fancy for dinner, and where the money should be spent. Life is more fun when it is combined with another. By the same token, a good significant other supports their partner. In healthy relationships, there is a wonderful to and fro of reliance. But people with Dependent Personality Disorder slide down the relationship slope. They are incapable of being there for others. Their needs are too great and require constant approval and reassurance from others. They lose their decision-making skills, and thus are unable to be independent. Their low self-esteem makes them fearful of separation, clinging from one relationship to another. The ultimate need is to be in a relationship, any relationship. As a result, they tend to find themselves in damaging relationships. Women with this disorder often endure unhealthy and abusive relationships, while men who suffer from this disorder tend to try to mask their fundamental need for dependence by acting demanding and pushy.

The dependent wife displays her excessive reliance by becoming needy and clingy. What would you like for dinner? What should I wear to the reception? Are these cookies all right for the PTA meeting? Does this laundry detergent get your shirts clean enough? On and on. A dependent wife will not only allow her husband to make all the household decisions, she'll beg him to. No decision is too trivial or too domestic to defer to her man. After all, when your sense of self is derived exclusively from your relationship with your husband, you have no confidence in your ability to make any decisions and are fearful of ever losing the source of approval.

The dependent husband is so fearful of losing his spouse that he tries to control everything about her. He will tell her what to eat, what to wear and who to talk to. Some men even make their partners wear glasses so she would not be so attractive to others.

Have you ever seen relationships between an absolutely gorgeous woman and a rather Plain Jane friend or the rugged football captain with a member of his entourage who is a sycophant? These relationships are based on domination and submission, on fear and self-loathing. The submissive friend relies on the reflected glory of the more accomplished friend,

while the more accomplished friend relies on the reassuring certainty of having a groupie for a friend. Perhaps you know someone like this.

The following quiz explores the characteristics of Dependent Personality Disorder.

Unequal relationships, such as the one with the clingy wife or submissive friend, grow from the Dependant Personality Disorder sufferer's abject fear of

DO YOU HAVE DEPENDENT PERSONALITY DISORDER?

Remember it is fine, even preferable, to rely on your mate—provided it is a two-way street. You may have Dependent Personality Disorder if you have an excessive need to be mollycoddled and you do at least five of the following:

1. You can't make everyday decisions without consulting others.

2. You need others to take responsibility for major parts of your life.

3. You struggle to disagree with those who support you.

4. You struggle to start tasks without others helping you.

5. You need the approval of others so badly you end up doing things you find unpleasant.

6. You feel uncomfortable when alone because you grow convinced you cannot fend for yourself.

7. You start a new relationship as soon as you are out of the old one.

8. You frequently worry what will happen if there is no one to take care of you.

separation. This fear stems from childhood. It is up to the parents to promise the child that they will return and then, when they do, to go to the child and say, "See, I kept my promise. I love you. I will not abandon you." It is not an easy lesson to learn, but if we can, then we are able to use the experience to become individuals who embrace the world and healthy relationships.

It is the lack of self-esteem that causes individuals to become irrationally dependent on others. While we have seen some Dependent Personality Disorders manifest themselves in Gollum-like behavior, there are other manifestations of these personality disorders which are not as easy to identify.

MR. DEPENDABLE

Take, for example, old Mr. Dependable. He's the fellow who, when you ask for a ride to the airport at 9:00, is comfortably parked at your curbside at 8:45, just to be sure that he is not late. At first glance, you might think of Mr. Dependable as just being a really nice guy. But, in fact, he is acting out the same fear of separation drama that any four-year-old participates in when the babysitter arrives. His behavior practically screams out, "Like me. *Please* like me!"

MISS NEEDS-TO-PLEASE

Like Mr. Dependable, there are those who simply "need to please." They will go to absurd lengths to keep everyone happy. Conflict frightens Miss Needs-to-Please because she knows that, when the dust settles, someone will be mad—and maybe at her. So, rather than tempt fate, they will try to please. For them, every molehill has the potential to be an Everest, a very unsettling and threatening thought.

MRS. NEEDS-TO-CONTROL

Whatever faults Mr. Dependable and Miss Needs-to-Please might have, there is one thing you can say for them: They are helpful to have around, not like Mrs. Needs-to-Control, who can make your life hell. Like the others, fear is at the root of her maddening personality. She just has to be in control of every decision—where to go, what to do, at work or at play—she will make the decisions. Loss of control evokes the painful memories of when she felt abandoned and alone. Control, and control at all costs, is the way she wards off that horrible pain of separation.

All of these personality traits emanate from the same problem—low self-esteem. While low self-esteem has become a popular excuse to explain away everything from bedwetting to the inability to balance a checkbook, the fact is that those who truly suffer from low self-esteem have real problems.

We all exist at varying points on a spectrum of self-confidence. We tend to be more confident about those things we are good at and less confident about those things we are not. An actor might not avoid public speaking, but may cringe at the thought of trying to hit a baseball. Someone with a wonderful voice will be confident singing, while a tone-deaf plumber might want to limit his vocal exercises to the shower. A lack of confidence is not the same thing as low self-esteem. Confidence is the ability to *do* something. Self-esteem is rooted in the need to *be* someone. When a person with low self-esteem performs, it is generally to gain acceptance and approval.

People with a healthy sense of self can be involved in a relationship on equal footing with their partners, knowing that, at times, one will be more dominant than the other. But people with Dependent Personality Disorder need approval too much to risk the kind of honesty that allows relationships—and people—to grow.

TEST YOURSELF

Instructions

To better understand your own self-image, take the test below. The test has been broken into two sections. Questions 1 to 20 ask you to evaluate *how important* certain aspects of life are to your self-esteem. Questions 21 to 40 ask you to evaluate your *satisfaction* with various elements of your self and experience.

Answer each question using a 0 to 10 scale, where 0 means "no importance at all" and 10 means "extremely important." While this is easy to complete, a word of warning: This is a very provocative test. Your results will ping at your emotions. If you are honest with your answers, you are going to get a glaring reflection in the results. It is best to do this test alone, and you can decide later whether to share your answers. Don't rush this one.

Please indicate how *important* the following are in your life:

	Not Important at All						Extremely Important			
1. Looks and physical attractiveness	0 1 2 3 4 5 6 7 8 9 10
2. Physical condition, strength, agility	0 1 2 3 4 5 6 7 8 9 10
3. Grooming, clothing, overall appearance	0 1 2 3 4 5 6 7 8 9 10
4. Being liked by others, your popularity and ability to get along, your social skills	0 1 2 3 4 5 6 7 8 9 10
5. Intelligence, how smart you are	0 1 2 3 4 5 6 7 8 9 10
6. Level of academic accomplishment, years of education	0 1 2 3 4 5 6 7 8 9 10
7. Being a cultured and knowledgeable person, knowing about art, music, world events	0 1 2 3 4 5 6 7 8 9 10
8. Having special talents or abilities—artistic, scientific, musical, athletic, etc	0 1 2 3 4 5 6 7 8 9 10
9. Earning a great amount of money and acquiring valuable possessions	0 1 2 3 4 5 6 7 8 9 10
10. Being recognized for your accomplishments, earning the respect of others for your work	0 1 2 3 4 5 6 7 8 9 10

	Not Important at All									Extremely Important
11. Doing what you set out to do personally, meeting the goals you set for yourself	0	1	2	3	4	5	6	7	8	9	10
12. Having influence over the events or people in your life	0	1	2	3	4	5	6	7	8	9	10
13. Being a good person, your friendliness and helpfulness to others	0	1	2	3	4	5	6	7	8	9	10
14. Being a law-abiding, responsible citizen	0	1	2	3	4	5	6	7	8	9	10
15. Being an honest and truthful person in your dealings with others	0	1	2	3	4	5	6	7	8	9	10
16. Having the courage of your convictions, speaking up for what you think is right, even when it is not popular to do so	0	1	2	3	4	5	6	7	8	9	10
17. Relationships with your family, being on good terms with your family, having good feelings for each other	0	1	2	3	4	5	6	7	8	9	10
18. Meeting or having met your responsibilities to your family, i.e., being a good parent, spouse, son, or daughter	0	1	2	3	4	5	6	7	8	9	10
19. Having a loving, close relationship with someone	0	1	2	3	4	5	6	7	8	9	10
20. Belief in a higher power, your spiritual convictions	0	1	2	3	4	5	6	7	8	9	10

Fleming, J.S. and Elovson, A. The Adult Sources of Self-Esteem Scale. Used by permission.

For the next set of questions, use the same 0 to 10 scale, but now 0 means "Not Satisfied at All" and 10 means "Extremely Satisfied."

Please indicate how *satisfied* you are with your:

	Not Satisfied							Extremely Satisfied			
1. Looks and physical attractiveness	0	1	2	3	4	5	6	7	8	9	10
2. Physical condition, strength, agility	0	1	2	3	4	5	6	7	8	9	10
3. Grooming, clothing, overall appearance	0	1	2	3	4	5	6	7	8	9	10
4. Being liked by others, your popularity and ability to get along, your social skills	0	1	2	3	4	5	6	7	8	9	10
5. Intelligence, how smart you are	0	1	2	3	4	5	6	7	8	9	10
6. Level of academic accomplishment, years of education	0	1	2	3	4	5	6	7	8	9	10
7. Being a cultured and knowledgeable person, knowing about art, music, world events	0	1	2	3	4	5	6	7	8	9	10
8. Having special talents or abilities—artistic, scientific, musical, athletic, etc.	0	1	2	3	4	5	6	7	8	9	10
9. Earning a great amount of money and acquiring valuable possessions	0	1	2	3	4	5	6	7	8	9	10

	Not Satisfied									Extremely Satisfied	
10. Being recognized for your accomplishments, earning the respect of others for your work	0	1	2	3	4	5	6	7	8	9	10
11. Doing what you set out to do personally, meeting the goals you set for yourself	0	1	2	3	4	5	6	7	8	9	10
12. Having influence over the events or people in your life	0	1	2	3	4	5	6	7	8	9	10
13. Being a good person, your friendliness and helpfulness to others	0	1	2	3	4	5	6	7	8	9	10
14. Being a law-abiding, responsible citizen	0	1	2	3	4	5	6	7	8	9	10
15. Being an honest and truthful person in your dealings with others	0	1	2	3	4	5	6	7	8	9	10
16. Having the courage of your convictions, speaking up for what you think is right, even when it is not popular to do so	0	1	2	3	4	5	6	7	8	9	10
17. Relationships with your family, being on good terms with your family, having good feelings for each other	0	1	2	3	4	5	6	7	8	9	10
18. Meeting or having met your responsibilities to your family, i.e., being a good parent, spouse, son, or daughter	0	1	2	3	4	5	6	7	8	9	10
19. Having a loving, close relationship with someone	0	1	2	3	4	5	6	7	8	9	10
20. Belief in a higher power, your spiritual convictions	0	1	2	3	4	5	6	7	8	9	10

Scoring Your Test

This clever test measures your self-esteem across seven different areas. To score your results, subtract the number you circled in the first part from your number in the second part of the test. For example, if you felt that your looks and attractiveness were a 6 on the importance scale, and gave them a 4 on the satisfaction scale, subtract 4 from 6 and enter 2 below. Notice that sometimes, if you are more satisfied on a less important question, you can get a negative score. That's okay, write down the negative number.

DIFFERENCE SCORES
Your Outward Self: How You Are Seen by Others.

Appearance and Popularity   **Difference**
1. Looks and physical attractiveness

2. Physical condition, strength, agility

3. Grooming, clothing, overall appearance

4. Being liked by others, your popularity and ability to get along, your social skills

Intellect and Abilities   **Difference**
5. Intelligence, how smart you are

6. Level of academic accomplishment, years of education

7. Being a cultured and knowledgeable person, knowing about art, music, world events

8. Having special talents or abilities—artistic, scientific, musical, athletic, etc.

Personal Achievement and Recognition   **Difference**

9. Earning a great amount of money and acquiring valuable possessions

----

10. Being recognized for your accomplishments, earning the respect of others for your work

----

11. Doing what you set out to do personally, meeting the goals you set for yourself

- -

Your Personal Self: How You See Yourself

Personal Control   **Difference**

12. Having influence over the events or people in your life

Ethics and Integrity   **Difference**

13. Being a good person, your friendliness and helpfulness to others

----

14. Being a law-abiding, responsible citizen

----

15. Being an honest and truthful person in your dealings with others

----

16. Having the courage of your convictions, speaking up for what you think is right, even when it is not popular to do so

----

Relationships   **Difference**

17. Relationships with your family, being on good terms with your family, having good feelings for each other

----

18. Meeting or having met your responsibilities to your family, i.e., being a good parent, spouse, son, or daughter

----

Relationships	Difference
19. Having a loving, close relationship with someone	

Spirituality	Difference
20. Belief in a higher power, your spiritual convictions	

- -

UNDERSTANDING YOUR SCORE

If you feel a category is important, yet you are dissatisfied with your score on it, this can indicate low self-esteem. The bigger the numeric difference between the first part and the second part of the test, the greater possibility of lower self-esteem. Difference scores of more than 3 or 4 within a category suggest areas for attention. Conversely, negative scores indicate areas where you are more satisfied than it is important to you, which may be a wasted effort. Consider each answer carefully. For those areas where differences are great, think: On what did you base your conclusion? Is your source internal or external? Take a step back and look at the two main sections: your outward self and your personal self.

Impostors

Our sense of self, of who we are, is essential to our understanding of ourselves and our place in the world. Still, the truth is most of us are "impostors" to some degree. We exaggerate our exploits in business. We minimize our shortcomings to friends. We present to the world something we're not, if only because we want to be accepted by the world and people around us. This is natural and normal. However, there are some conditions of the mind in which we find ourselves doing a lot more than simply shading the truth.

FOREIGN ACCENT SYNDROME

Imagine what your family would say if you showed up at the breakfast table and greeted them with a, " 'ello, luv!" What might your coworkers think? What would *you* think if you suddenly found yourself speaking with a foreign accent? Impossible, you say? Not for a Philadelphia native, when she woke up one fine day in 1999 speaking with a British accent. Despite the insistence of her family and coworkers, she was neither faking it nor practicing for a Monty Python skit. She had no control over her accent. She could only speak like a Brit. This proved to be neither enjoyable nor amusing for the victim of this strange disorder. After a period of terrible confusion and embarrassment, she changed her name and moved in order to begin anew with a simulated identity that would match her accent.

So, what's going on here? If sufferers from this disorder aren't mimicking foreign actors, why are they speaking so funny? According to Oxford neuropsychologists, when there is damage to the left hemisphere of the brain, where language processing takes place, it can lead to a rare speech disorder known as Foreign Accent Syndrome. A stroke or a whack to the head makes patients change their pronunciation to sound like nonnative speakers.

It was just such a whack in the head which triggered the first reported case of Foreign Accent Syndrome in 1941. A young Norwegian woman suffered shrapnel injuries to the brain during a Luftwaffe air raid. Upon her initial recovery, she suffered with severe language problems. She recovered from these, but was left with what sounded like a

Foreign Accent Syndrome can make you think you are losing your mind.

pronounced German accent. Such an accent was particularly unwelcome during the war and the young woman, after already suffering so much, was ostracized by her community.

Those who suffer from Foreign Accent Syndrome often feel as if they are losing their minds until they learn that there is a very real physical reason for their strange behavior. Although there is no indication that this syndrome can be cured, just knowing that they are not losing their minds is of great comfort to sufferers of this malady.

Feeling Like an Impostor?

Foreign Accent Syndrome is but one of several disorders in which we find our minds not belonging to our bodies. There are times when people find they are strangers to themselves—they fail to see the person the rest of the world perceives. They look into a mirror and cannot see the image of who is there, but rather, they see the image of someone who *should* be there. To the impostor, the reflection in the mirror is like a thief who has stolen the real them. And they will do whatever it takes to get their real selves back. Anything at all.

BODY INTEGRITY IDENTITY DISORDER

Our tour has taken us to the minds of many individuals. Ideally, some of the personalities we met reminded you of friends and family and provided you with a few "aha" moments as you linked individuals to peculiar behavior. Now that we are getting near the end of the tour, I feel compelled to take you to a very dark place. A small community with a disturbing, alarming secret. Everyone I met in this tiny town is polite and kind, but I warn you, their needs are not for the queasy. Welcome to Body Integrity Identity Disorder.

Those with BIID absolutely believe that their bodies
are not right because they possess an extra limb.

Where the other maladies we visited exist somewhere in gray
area between normal and abnormal, Body Integrity Identity Disorder (BIID) is a black or white disorder that exists on the far-
thest rim of the darkness.

People with BIID absolutely believe that their bodies are not
right because they possess an extra limb. Not, mind you, delu-
sional individuals who are upset because they think they have a
third arm or those who actually *do* have an extra appendage. We
are talking about individuals who want to have normal, fully
functioning parts of their bodies cut off. They are amputee
wannabes—otherwise-fine individuals who, in order to have
their bodies physically match their mental image of their perfect
selves, need to chop off their arms or legs.

If you speak with amputee wannabes, you will discover individuals who are articulate, often intelligent, and absolutely certain that their "true selves" can exist only after the removal of a limb. These people speak with the same candor and determination as those who seek sex-reassignment surgery. They are simply "not who they are supposed to be" with their limbs intact. Take, for example, the gentleman from Liverpool, England. He was a four-year-old boy when he first saw an amputee. (It seems that most people with BIID had a very early exposure to an amputee that became indelibly written in their minds.) By the time he was a child of seven he began to think: "This is how I *should* be." The feeling followed him throughout his life. It was not, however, until he was in his fifties that he actually had his leg amputated.

Unable to find a surgeon willing to perform the surgery, he froze his leg in dry ice until it was irreversibly damaged and then

THE SECRET CODE OF AMPUTATION WANNABES

Those who feel the need to remove all or parts of their limbs use a shorthand to describe the offending body part. Here are examples of some codes.

rak (right leg above knee)

lbk (left leg below knee)

rbk (right leg below knee)

lak (left leg above knee)

rbe (right arm below elbow)

lbe (left leg below elbow)

rae (right arm above elbow)

lae (left arm above elbow)

was able to persuade a surgeon to remove the useless limb. When he awoke from the anesthetic and realized his left leg was really gone, he thought to himself, "All my torment has disappeared." While there are few documented statistics, apparently most wannabes are very pleased with the results of their amputations.

Wannabes often pretend to be amputees. At first, privately at home, one might use an Ace bandage to strap the lower leg to the thigh to feign being an rbk. Others will venture outside sporting crutches or an unnecessary prosthetic. Some tape fingers down for the session of impairment.

There is also a sexual element for many with this disorder. For some, the tenderness of sexual relations reduces the desire to remove the offending appendage. For others, the sight of true amputees is a real turn on.

Fake Pregnancies

While those with BIID may feel that they are impostors imprisoned in their own bodies, other forms of impostors are willing to go to extreme lengths to bring their bodies into congruence with their image of themselves. The majority of people with BIID are male, as are those who suffer from another impostor condition, fake pregnancy.

Fake pregnancy? It is possible to have some sympathy and understanding for females who struggle with this disorder. After all, in a culture and society that elevates the status of motherhood to almost spiritual levels, an inability to become pregnant can translate into a terrible sense of failure. That some women, reacting to this sense of failure, would cross the line and fake pregnancy seems worthy of our sympathy and understanding. However, the desire by men to overcome the same inability evokes different emotions.

As one such gentleman wrote:

I've always fantasized about a woman who would be able to get me pregnant instead of the other way around. I have no idea where these particular fantasies come from. In some of my fantasies, having her baby is the ultimate way of showing my love. At other times, it is being used and made to risk getting pregnant against my will that is the turn-on. Maybe strange, but I find both of these ideas intensely erotic!

Unless pregnant, these individuals feel as though they are not really themselves. To bring their body image in line with the person they expect to see looking back in the mirror, they go through elaborate disguises to create the impression of pregnancy.

Small beach balls filled with varying amounts of water correspond to how they would look throughout a successful pregnancy. Their balls are attached to their stomachs with elastic bandages. The men who emulate pregnancy know that they are neither pregnant nor female. However, in pretending, they bring their bodies more in line with the image of themselves that they hold to be true. Of course, there are female impostors who perform the same elaborate simulations.

Intellectual Impostors

Do you know a bright, hardworking, wonderful person who is plagued with self-doubt? It seems the harder they work, the more of a phony they feel? These are intellectual impostors. Intelligent knowledgeable folks who feel that they are undeserved of the credit they receive. I want to make it clear that these are not slackers who have cheated their way through school and lied on their resumes. These are diligent, scrupulous individuals who believe their success is a sham. This phenomenon is more common in successful women.

TEST YOURSELF

Instructions

We are all impostors to some degree. We all wear masks. Many of us feel that our success in life is just a façade, that we are masquerading our way through life. Do you feel like an original or a fake?

The questions on this test are simple—they focus on thoughts that pass through our minds. To answer each of the twenty statements just circle the number that best shows how often you have each thought. Don't dwell on this. Just go with your first instinct and you will be done in five minutes.

Please circle the first response that enters your mind and circle the corresponding number.

	Not at All True	Rarely	Sometimes	Often	Very True
1. I have often succeeded on a test or task even though I was afraid that I would not do well before I undertook the task.	1	2	3	4	5
2. I can give the impression that I'm more competent than I really am.	1	2	3	4	5
3. I avoid evaluations if possible and have a dread of others evaluating me.	1	2	3	4	5
4. When people praise me for something I've accomplished, I'm afraid I won't be able to live up to their expectations of me in the future.	1	2	3	4	5
5. I sometimes think I obtained my present position or gained my present success because I happened to be in the right place at the right time or knew the right people.	1	2	3	4	5
6. I'm afraid people important to me may find out that I'm not as capable as they think I am.	1	2	3	4	5
7. I tend to remember the incidents in which I have not done my best more than those times I have done my best.	1	2	3	4	5

	Not at All True	Rarely	Sometimes	Often	Very True
8. I rarely do a project or task as well as I'd like to do it.	1	2	3	4	5
9. Sometimes I feel or believe that my success in my life or in my job has been the result of some kind of error.	1	2	3	4	5
10. It's hard for me to accept compliments or praise about my intelligence or accomplishments.	1	2	3	4	5
11. At times, I feel my success was due to some kind of luck.	1	2	3	4	5
12. I'm disappointed at times in my present accomplishments and think I should have accomplished much more.	1	2	3	4	5
13. Sometimes, I'm afraid others will discover how much knowledge or ability I really lack.	1	2	3	4	5
14. I'm often afraid that I may fail at a new assignment or undertaking even though I generally do well at what I attempt.	1	2	3	4	5
15. When I've succeeded at something and received recognition for my accomplishments, I have doubts that I can keep repeating that success.	1	2	3	4	5
16. If I receive a great deal of praise and recognition for something I've accomplished, I tend to discount the importance of what I have done.	1	2	3	4	5

	Not at All True	Rarely	Sometimes	Often	Very True
17. I often compare my ability to those around me and think they may be more intelligent than I am.	1	2	3	4	5
18. I often worry about not succeeding with a project or on an examination, even though others around me have considerable confidence that I will do well.	1	2	3	4	5
19. If I'm going to receive a promotion or gain recognition of some kind, I hesitate to tell others until it is an accomplished fact.	1	2	3	4	5
20. I feel bad and discouraged if I'm not "the best" or at least "very special" in situations that involve achievement.	1	2	3	4	5

Clance, P.R. (1985). The Impostor Phenomenon: Overcoming the Fear that Haunts Your Success. Atlanta: Peachtree Publishers. Under copyright. Do not reproduce without permission of Pauline Rose Clance. Used by permission.

Scoring Your Test

To learn your score, simply add the numbers you circled and write the sum here:

Your Score: _____

WHAT DOES YOUR SCORE MEAN?

Your Score	Level of Impostor Feelings
Less than 31	Feelin' like an Original
31 to 40	Feelin' like the Real McCoy
41 to 60	Feelin' Legitimate
61 to 80	Feelin' like a Pretender
More than 80	Feelin' like a Phony

UNDERSTANDING YOUR SCORE

Score of Less than 40—What You See Is What You Get!

Great score! You have a realistic view of your success and which situations are within your control. You are a down-to-earth, genuine person who, as the saying goes, feels comfortable in your own skin. You take credit when it is due for your hard work and you're probably gracious when you make errors, too.

Score of 41 to 60—What You See Is Fairly Accurate!

Good job. While you have some feelings of inadequacy, you generally have a pretty accurate view of your successes and accomplishments. Occasionally, you wrestle with concerns that you will be discovered as a fake or phony and that perhaps your education will be discredited, but you earned those achievements and deserve a little swagger when you feel good about them.

Scores—61 or More—What You See Is a Big Phony!

You are plagued with feelings of inadequacy and that your successes in life are somehow not under your control. You push yourself incredibly hard to obtain success, but once it's obtained, you discount your effort and ascribe accomplishments to luck. Deep-seated feelings of intellectual phoniness plague people who score in this category. You probably secretly fear that one day you will be tested or found out to be a worthless fake. Oddly, although you feel like a charlatan at times, it is the genuine nature of your personality that is penalized because of your skewed view. Interestingly, research shows that no matter how many times you are successful based on your own abilities, you will not weaken the impostor feelings. If you would like to reduce these feelings of fraud, tackle the problem by reviewing your self-esteem test results, set short-term, realistic goals for yourself, and discuss your perceptions openly with those you trust to be honest sounding boards.

Narcolepsy

As daylight wanes and we draw near the end of our tour, let's visit our remaining personalities in their sleep.

Imagine: You're in the passenger seat. It is dusk. The windows are rolled down and the warm breeze rushes in, blowing back your hair. Music is playing on the radio. You turn to say something to the driver. He nods. Then he nods again and, to your terror, you realize that he's fallen asleep!

"Hey!" you scream, reaching out and punching his shoulder.

He raises his head and opens his eyes. "Huh? What? What's the matter?"

"You just fell asleep!"

You have just been introduced to narcolepsy, a disabling neurological disorder that disrupts sleep regulation. More specifically, it is an intrusion of rapid eye movement (REM) sleep, the dreaming state of sleep, into wakefulness. For most sufferers, symptoms first show up between the ages of fifteen and thirty. Narcoleptics may also experience disturbed sleep during the night, tossing and turning in bed, leg jerks, nightmares, and frequent awakenings.

This is not a falling-asleep-at-the-opera disorder as the nar-

Sleep attacks can occur at any time.

coleptic cannot keep his eyes open. This is not the woman who dozes as soon as the television comes on. No. This is mind control with the mind losing. This is the gentleman driving along the freeway at sixty-five miles an hour feeling chipper as an eighteen-year-old whose eyes suddenly droop and, for a few seconds, falls asleep. This is the woman who is at her desk at work, actually enjoying the particular challenge posed by the task at hand, who is suddenly out like a light.

Too often, people who are witness to a narcoleptic event will

DO YOU HAVE NARCOLEPSY?

There are five classic symptoms of narcolepsy. If you answer yes to these four questions, speak to your physician.

Have you experienced overpowering bouts of refreshing sleep daily for the past three months?	YES NO
When this happens, do you experience cataplexy (sudden, brief episodes of muscle weakness or paralysis usually brought on by laughter, anticipation, or anger)?	YES NO
When this happens, do you experience paralysis upon falling asleep or waking up or hallucinations (extremely vivid, dreamlike images that accompany sleep onset)?	YES NO
Is this disturbance not due to substance abuse or medication?	YES NO

presume that the person simply didn't get a good night's sleep the night before. But length and quality of nighttime sleep have nothing to do with this malady. Narcolepsy has nothing to do with being tired. The embarrassing and limited nature of sleep attacks erode the quality of life for this incurable condition.

Nightmares

You wake up screaming. You are covered in sweat. Your heart is racing. You are trembling. You have managed to wake yourself up just before, a) you fell off the cliff, b) the masked men burst into the room, guns a'blazing, or c) a multi-headed beast with dripping fangs had sniffed you out at the back of the darkened cave—take your pick. The bottom line is that you have had a nightmare.

Nightmares are terrifying dreams that jar the sleeper from REM sleep. Some people refer to nightmares as "dream anxiety attacks" because they elicit the same kind of emotional and physical response as an anxiety attack. The sleeper is suddenly awakened with intense fear, anxiety, and, very often, a feeling of doom. Wakefulness is immediate and complete. (Unlike a night terror, in which you remain essentially asleep throughout.) What's more, the details of the nightmare are intensely vivid, unlike a pleasant dream, which seems to recede the moment you return to consciousness.

Although nightmares are reasonably common, they are experiences that not only fall under the category of nighttime quirks, but they also make clear that there are times when, for all our efforts, we are not in control of the things that happen in our minds. If nightmares disturb sleep to the extent that it interferes with your ability to function each day, you may have Nightmare Disorder.

Somnambulism, or Sleepwalking

Few things are freakier than to come upon someone sharpening knives—only to discover that they are sound asleep! It does make you wonder whether to carefully ask for the knives or to slowly retreat from the room and hope for the best.

Sleepwalking in children is most likely related to fatigue, prior sleep loss, or even anxiety. In adults, sleepwalking is usually associated with a disorder of the mind, but may also be seen with reactions to drugs and alcohol, or medical conditions. In the elderly, sleepwalking may be a symptom of an organic brain syndrome or REM behavior disorders.

A sleepwalking episode can last anywhere from a few seconds to thirty minutes—more than enough time to get dressed, go out to the car and drive to get the paper.

Circadian Rhythm Sleep Disorder

We are veritable biological clock stores. Circadian Rhythm Sleep Disorder is the result of our internal twenty-four-hour clock being thrown out-of-whack. Jet travel is a prime cause of this disorder, sending people into time zones that are out of kilter with the one that their internal clocks expect. "Jet lag" is a common expression of this disorder.

It is not just jet travel that has thrown us off, however. Since Edison invented the light bulb, our biological clocks have been going out of sync. Our sleep patterns are no longer dictated by the rising and the setting of the sun, but rather by artificial means, such as how funny your late night TV show was. Naturally, this can throw our sleep cycles into disarray and make us feel groggy and tired during what should be our waking hours.

Losing Our Grasp

Ultimately, these sleep disorders, like the other issues identified in this chapter, blur the line between what is fantasy and what is reality. After all, is the sleepwalker in more or less control of his life than the woman who fakes pregnancy or the man who amputates his arm in order to feel fully himself?

The more we delve into mind-control issues—from dependent personalities to nightmares—the more we must acknowledge that we not only wear masks to protect who we really are, but we also drape masks over the world around us, effectively altering reality according to our inner sense of what should be there.

8.

the big picture: your place in the world

Let us not look back in anger, nor forward in fear, but around in awareness. —JAMES THURBER

Human personalities are so complex that we will never completely understand them. There are simply too many variables involved. The best we can do is classify and label them. As a people, we have made great strides in comprehending genetics, atomic physics, and the nature of the cosmos. But we have little knowledge of who we are—or more specifically, why we are the way we are. We have visited over eighty personality "disorders" in the past two hundred–odd pages. We've labeled them and described them. But, we still don't know why a young woman would choose to cut her arms with a razor any more than why an old man would believe he should surgically remove a perfectly fine limb. Heck, we don't even know why people sort their M&Ms by color or why successful people feel like failures. Human behavior remains a fascinating mystery.

As we reach the end of our personality tour, I'd like you to step back a bit and look at the big picture. We will back away one step at a time, looking at how personality affects you, other individuals, culture, and, finally, the world.

Let's start with you. We have peered into your mind with eighteen scientific tests. Ideally, you have approached these honestly and have come away with a little insight into the most complex, but most personal, aspects of your life. Of course there is the question: Now that I've learned my score, what can I do about it? Two options: If you are pleased with your score and you feel that this section of your personality is in order, great! If, on the other hand, you wish to change your personality in some ways, that is great too. Again, you have two options: acceptance and change. Accepting yourself for all of your strengths and weaknesses is a cornerstone to lifelong happiness. You don't have to change unless you want to change. One hidden secret about personality is that you can revamp it. However, altering your personality is not like winning the lottery or going in for an instant makeover. You don't spend a little, then suddenly get a boat load of change. Developing your personality is more like a health program where you slowly change your diet, flex different muscles, sweat a little, vary your routine. You will develop, but it takes time and a concerted effort.

Also keep in mind that many quirks are nature's protective mechanisms gone a little askew. We saw a pattern. Generally, we consider it good to have a little of each trait. Take jealousy, for example. Jealousy has evolved with humans to make us protective of something extremely important—our relationships. Too little jealousy and you have a laissez-faire relationship, too much and you have the crush of a relationship killer. This pattern continues throughout most of the characteristics we've spied on.

While we are talking about you, let's mention your relationships. We saw that to be human is to relate. We need others for survival. No man is an island. To that end, it is marvelous fun to take these tests with loved ones. Many of them are wonderful to do in bed. Sit in bed with your partner and take the tests individually. From here, you can either play a little guessing game on how your partner scored, or "swap personalities" and take the test pretending to be your partner. Maybe I've been looking into minds too long, but I find a little role reversal is a real treat.

If you are really adventurous, you can use *Are You Crazy?* at parties. Gather your friends around, give them a pen and paper, choose a test, and start asking the questions. From the delights of the Narcissism to the quiet contemplation of the Impostor test, having a group go through a few quizzes is a lot of fun. I wrote a companion book to *Are You Crazy?* called *How Do You Compare?* (Perigee) which is also perfect for parties.

Alright, enough about you, let's talk about those with bizarre behavior. The book provides a little taste or snippet of over eighty personality quirks. A smorgasbord of strangeness is served to give you a flavor of the range of behavior outside your door. While formal diagnosis of many conditions is rare, (because an individual has to be so plagued by a problem that they cannot function well), I guarantee that you know people with lighter shades of some of them. We all have friends, family members, and colleagues that exhibit hints of some symptoms. This is a good thing. Life would be incredibly boring if we all thought the same, reacted the same, and behaved the same. It is the uniqueness of our personalities that provides color and texture to the tapestry of our culture.

We need to foster greater understanding of others. The National Institute for Mental Health estimates that more than one in five American adults will be diagnosed with a mental disorder this year. That is a lot of people. Good people. We understand when someone we work with gets a cold and has to take a few days off. We know the cause, the symptoms, we know they may become cranky and their noses may run. We understand and accept them. This is not always the case with mental illness. We don't always understand, we don't always accept.

I lost my high school sweetheart, my beautiful wife, and the mother of my three terrific children to mental illness. Watching her sweet, caring, loving mind fade away was horrific. The only positive thing I got out of it was a modicum of understanding. I want to share that with you in her memory. If, while reading this book, you recognized someone close to you, show them a kindness. Take a few steps in their shoes. Try to understand. Try to accept.

It is always important to understand that definitions of mental well-being vary by culture. As George Carlin wrote: "Those who dance are considered insane by those who can't hear the music."

Earlier, we saw that as a society, we consider those who cut and burn themselves as having a problem. But why are those who stab holes and inject dye into their bodies considered artistic? Have you seen people with pins through their ears, eyebrows, tongue, chin, and cheeks? How about those covered with tattoos? Our society considers body piercing and getting tattoos as socially acceptable behaviors, not symptoms of a mental disturbance. But it does make you wonder . . .

Along that same vein, a common reaction to learning about BIID is repulsion. Why? Because it is difficult to comprehend why someone would want to remove a perfectly healthy body part. Hmmmm . . . how does what these people do differ from more acceptable forms of self-mutilation? According to the American Society for Aesthetic Plastic Surgery, over nine million Americans will have perfectly healthy body parts altered in 2005 alone. As a society, we freely permit (some would say encourage) those who are unhappy with their noses, breasts, and bellies to have them removed, reshaped, restyled, remodeled, and restructured.

Why? Because these areas of the body do not match their owner's perception of how they want them to look. And let us not forget the parents of 1.2 million perfectly healthy baby boys who will have their foreskins removed this year. Perhaps we should consider all members of our society before condemning a few.

Our culture plays a similar game with schizophrenia. There are those who hear voices in their heads and shout nonsense then get labeled as mentally ill, while others with the same conditions are praised for their religious conviction and for speaking in tongues. As a society, we sometimes find ourselves traveling on thin ground.

Histrionic Personality Disorder

As we take the biggest step back and look at what constitutes mental health in other nations, I want to share another cross-cultural psychiatric problem. Histrionic Personality Disorder could be considered the "over-actor" ailment. Individuals with this problem demand to be the center of attention—they are flirtatious, shallow, and easily influenced. However, the checklist that determines whether you have this condition, like many others, varies by country. The two boxes below show as much about societal nuances as they do this disorder.

Personality Disorders Around the World

Now let's finish our tour of human idiosyncrasies by going international.

DO YOU HAVE HISTRIONIC PERSONALITY DISORDER? (UNITED STATES VERSION)

In the United States, you may have Histrionic Personality Disorder if you answer "yes" to at least five of these eight questions:

Do you become uncomfortable when you are not the center of attention?   YES NO

Do you use your appearance to draw attention to yourself?   YES NO

Do you tend to be seductive or sexually provocative with others?   YES NO

Do you tend to consider relationships as more intimate than they really are?   YES NO

Do your emotions quickly change?   YES NO

Are you overly dramatic and exaggerate your emotions?   YES NO

Is your style of speech excessively indistinct and lacking detail?   YES NO

Are you suggestible and easily influenced by others?   YES NO

TAIJIN KYOFUSHO

In what must be the antithesis to Histrionic Personality Disorder, Japanese psychiatrists have diagnosed a syndrome that includes intense fear that areas of one's body, facial expressions, odors, or movements greatly offend others.

DHAT

If you suffer with extreme anxiety about ejaculation and white urine, Dhat can be tough. Additional symptoms for this condition from India include weakness and exhaustion.

SHENKUI

While we are on the topic of semen, men should take note that in China you can lose your life force and become dizzy, fatigued, and weak due to excessive masturbation.

KORO

Ladies, take note. You are not immune from genital concerns. In many parts of Asia, both men and women suffer with episodes of extreme anxiety that their penis, vulva, or nipples will recede into the body and cause death.

MAL DE OJO

Women and children are more often stricken with mal de ojo or "the evil eye." If you are given the evil eye, symptoms include crying, diarrhea, and vomiting.

BRAIN FAG

If you are reading this book in Western Africa, it may give you brain fag, a condition experienced by students who think too much. Symptoms include difficulty concentrating, remembering, and thinking.

Conclusion

I hope you have enjoyed our romp around the mind and perhaps have come away with a better understanding of how we label mental illness and a little insight to what life is like for those with these labels. If you have a personality story to share or would like to say hello, please feel free to drop me a note at Andrew@howdoyoucompare.com. While I cannot promise to respond to all letters, I will read each one with interest.

Additionally, check out www.areyoucrazy.org for additional interesting tidbits.